SAILING SHIPS
AND SAILING CRAFT

The two primary causes that led to the evolution of sailing transport were the urges to migrate and to trade. Both led in turn to conflict, so there evolved three basic types of vessels: to carry migrants, to carry goods and for fighting.

The development of particular types of sailing vessels, as with other forms of evolution, was irregular. In some instances the process was a slow but steady forward movement through the centuries. Ideas were exchanged gradually and new designs adopted, often from widely differing sources. An outstanding example is provided by the sailing vessels of the eleventh and fourteenth centuries, in which the stability of the 'round ship' of the early Mediterranean peoples is combined with the seaworthiness and speed of the Norse longships.

This process of development continued into the nineteenth century, culminating perhaps in the clipper ships, which have been described as 'mankind's most beautiful creation'. On the other hand, while some ship forms underwent endless metamorphosis, other forms remained static: the Irish curragh has hardly changed in a thousand years, for example, while the galley has entirely disappeared.

We are grateful to the many institutions and individuals who have helped to make this book so authoritative. They are fully listed on page 156. The author adds his own appreciation for the unstinted help given by Captain A. V. Harris of Deal (a member of that exclusive brotherhood, 'The Cape Horners' Club').

A
GROSSET
ALL-COLOR GUIDE

SAILING SHIPS AND SAILING CRAFT

BY GEORGE GOLDSMITH-CARTER

Illustrated by Bill Robertshaw

GROSSET & DUNLAP
A NATIONAL GENERAL COMPANY
Publishers • New York

CONTENTS

SAILING VESSELS OF THE ANCIENT WORLD

Egypt

The origin of the sailing ship is lost in the mists of time, and the principle of the sail may have been discovered accidentally by some primitive man, seated on a drifting log, who noticed the effect of wind on his body. The earliest documented sailing ships seem to have been built by the Egyptians. In 1929 Sir Flinders Petrie unearthed a stone model of a sailing craft estimated to be 11,000 years old at Fayim. These vessels were essentially river craft, used only for sailing with the wind. Although they hated the sea, the Egyptians did build sea-going vessels, for around 2900 B.C. Pharaoh Sneferu assembled forty wooden ships and sent them to Byblos in Phoenicia to trade for cedar wood. They were without keels or frames, being built of short blocks of *acacia nilotica,* or sunt,

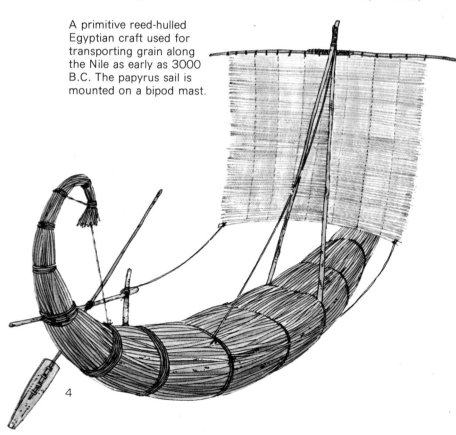

A primitive reed-hulled Egyptian craft used for transporting grain along the Nile as early as 3000 B.C. The papyrus sail is mounted on a bipod mast.

4

One of the fleet of wooden
ships, each steered by six oars,
assembled by Pharaoh Sneferu
c.2900 B.C. for trading purposes

pegged together like bricks. The bipod mast was counterbalanced with stones so that it could be lowered to the deck when the vessel was under oars. Steering was by six oars, while the purely non-functional stem- and sternposts were ornamented with the Eye of Horus and the Sacred Ankh, or Symbol of Life.

Bas reliefs of 1200 B.C. depict Rameses III's victory over the Philistines in the first known naval battle. They show warships with metal-shod rams. One powerful steering oar at the rear had now replaced the six individually manned oars described above. A single mast, conventionally stayed, carried

Warship of Rameses III,
with battering ram

the first 'fighting top'. The large, well-designed sails were brailed so that they could be furled without being lowered. High-planked bulwarks protected the rowers. These ships marked the zenith of ship building in ancient Egypt. Indeed, some Nile craft today are cruder than their ancient prototypes.

Ivory model of a boat found at Knossos.

Ancient Crete

As far as it can be established, the first people ever to build *seagoing* sailing vessels were the Neolithic inhabitants of Crete, who are known to have exported obsidian, a volcanic flint suitable for the manufacture of edged implements and weapons, to Egypt, as long ago as 3000 B.C. They also imported material from the Lipari Isles, near Sicily.

With the discovery of tin and copper and the advent of the Bronze Age, shipbuilding in the Mediterranean and the Near East received a tremendous stimulus, for the demand for these metals and for skilled metalworkers created the additional

Cretan ship engraved on a gold ring discovered at Mochlos.

Artist's impression of early Cretan trading vessels.

demand for capacious and seaworthy ships to carry them, as well as the metalware, pottery, skins, sponges, wine, olive oil and dried fish that Crete also exported. Thus the early Cretans built large fleets of trading vessels, loaded them with rich cargoes and sailed to every port in the Mediterranean, to the ports of Sicily, to Troy and to Egypt. Cretan ships with Cretan mariners now dominated sea commerce in the Mediterranean, the Adriatic and the Near East.

In 1908 an American archaeologist, Professor Seager, while excavating on the small, barren island of Mochlos, off Crete, unearthed a unique and splendid hoard of treasure, 4,500 years old. With the hoard was a massive gold ring which shows an engraving of a ship sailing from the shrine of Rhea, the Cretan mother-goddess who was also the protectress of sailors.

Sir Arthur Evans, while excavating the Great Palace of Knossos in Crete at the end of the nineteenth century, unearthed an ivory model of a sailing ship equipped with hold and hatch cover. He also discovered unique maritime seal stones; one such artifact of the Late Minoan Period (1700–1500 B.C.) was found during the excavation of the ruins of the royal villa near Knossos. It shows a single-masted ship carrying a horse and was considered by Sir Arthur Evans to record one of the first thoroughbred horses ever imported into Crete. Minoans probably sailed ships of the type depicted on these seal stones to establish their colony on the coast of Palestine about 1200 B.C.

Another steatite seal stone of the Early Minoan Period (2800–2200 B.C.) depicts a ship with two sails and with two crescent moons above the mast (perhaps to show that the voyage lasted two months). Other seals show vessels with one, two and even three masts; one found at Mirabello bears an engraving of a single-masted ship carrying a square sail and equipped with rigging of plaited ropes. Further ship finds in Crete included terracotta and alabaster models found by Italian archaeologists at Aghia Triadha near Phaestos in the vicinity of the Bay of Messara in southern Crete.

The Phoenicians

The Phoenicians left their racial cradle on the north coast of the Persian Gulf in approximately 200 B.C. to settle in Tyre and Sidon on the east coast of the Mediterranean. From here they sailed to colonize Cadiz, Carthage and Marseilles and the islands of Corsica and Sardinia, and started to compete with Cretan traders.

The Phoenicians, or Sidonians as they called themselves, built stout, seagoing sailing vessels of up to 300 tons' displace-

Phoenician trading ship

Phoenician war galley
equipped with narrow
'fighting platform'

ment. These had many of the features of both Cretan and
Egyptian ships, were single-masted and could only sail with
the wind, relying at other times on slave oarsmen. The stem-
posts were carved to resemble horses' heads, and the inward-
curving sternposts took the form of fishtails. Piracy was rife;
thus, Phoenician trading ships were always heavily armed.
The Phoenician warship was the bireme, a galley propelled by
two banks of oarsmen and carrying a square sail on a mast
stepped amidships. The most outstanding characteristic of
this shallow-draught, fast, maneuverable, but unseaworthy
vessel was the narrow fighting platform not unlike the 'cat-

Early Greek cargo vessel

walk' of a modern oil tanker. It also had a massive, horn-shaped ram.

The Phoenicians, who have been called the pioneers of the trade routes, sailed as far north as Britain for Cornish tin; but they were not true ocean venturers like the later Norsemen, preferring instead to hug the coast. It seems possible that they half believed their own horrific tales of sea monsters and supernatural beings, which they told to other seafarers in order to keep the secrets of the trade routes to themselves.

Ancient Greece and Rome
The ancient Greeks became sea-minded about 800 B.C. Like the Phoenicians, they founded overseas colonies. Much is known about their war galleys, but little about their trading vessels.

By the second century A.D. Mediterranean ship design had advanced considerably. Lucian, the Greek satirist, describes the *Isis,* a Roman grain ship he saw in Piraeus, Athens, in A.D. 150. This vessel was impressive: it was a fully decked ship with four big holds; its sternpost formed the head of a sacred Roman goose, and the bow bore the figurehead of the goddess Isis. Compare her dimensions with those of America's famous Cape Horn clipper *Great Republic*:

Isis: length 180ft.; beam 45–50ft.; holds 44ft. deep.
Great Republic: length 325ft.; beam 53ft.; holds 38ft. deep.

The disparity between the lengths and breadths of these ships shows the difference between the basic Mediterranean

The *Isis,* a broad-beamed
Roman grain carrier of the 2nd
century A.D.

'round-ship' form and the 'longship' form of the Northern sea peoples. Although characteristically Mediterranean, the 'round-ship' had a far-reaching influence on all future ships. The artemon (square bow sail) and awning-covered stern heralded the spritsail and ornate quarter-galleries of European galleons. The bow gallery was to become the forecastle of medieval ships, and the triangular topsails became the graceful 'moon-rakers' and 'kites' which crowned the Clipper ships.

MEDIEVAL SAILING SHIPS

Mediterranean ships of the Middle Ages

From the third century A.D. onward the history of shipbuilding in the Mediterranean is lost, but between the ninth and tenth centuries a revolutionary type of vessel appeared. Its hull was somewhat similar to the Cretan and Greek trading vessels: it was carvel-built (see pages 28–29), the bow raked forward and the stempost curved inward. However, the vessel carried two steering oars, and the well-stayed mast, stepped slightly forward of amidships and raked forward at an angle, had a peculiar hook-shaped masthead and carried a new type of sail, the 'lateen' (a European corruption of the word 'Latin').

The lateen—perhaps of Arab origin—was a right-angled

The Greek dromon, a heavily armored warship of the 12th century.

An early lateen-rigged ship, widely adopted in the 9th and 10th centuries A.D. by Mediterranean shipbuilders.

triangular sail laced to a long, sloping yard and controlled by a system of blocks and tackles which enabled the ship to sail against the wind. For the first time in history, sailing vessels which did not need oars appeared in the Mediterranean.

Nevertheless, the many-oared galley with its auxiliary sails was still generally used as a warship, although these too were beginning to change. By the beginning of the twelfth century the cumbersome trireme, with its three banks of oars and a ram, gave way to the formidable dromon (Greek *dromos* = runner).

13

The dromon carried up to three masts with lateen sails, and although equipped with two banks of oars, handled by 150 to 200 men, it also bore impressive heavy armament—*ballistae,* giant mechanically operated crossbows, which threw javelins, and *catapultae,* which hurled stone balls. Projecting from the bow was a bronze, bellows-operated Greek Fire projector. The armorer was called the *hataphaltaphetes.* Such were the warships used by the Saracens during the Crusades.

Skin boats of Ireland and the Arctic

The Eskimo umiak

These primitive craft were built by stretching ox-hides over sewn, or cloven, withe frames. They, like the Chinese junk, have altered little over the centuries—except that in more recent times the ox-hide covering was replaced by tarred calico. A small gold model of a curragh is part of the Broyghter Treasure Hoard, dated 200 B.C. The original was probably forty feet long, with a large ox-hide lug-type sail rigged to a rough tree-trunk mast and steered by a heavy oar rigged on the port quarter. The anchor—'killick'—was a long, heavy stone to which two wooden flukes were lashed.

Owing to its seaworthiness, lightness and speed, the sea-going sailing curragh was frequently used by the early Irish invaders of Britain. Chief of these was King Niall of the Nine Hostages, who ruled Ireland A.D. 379–405. He invaded Wales with such success that he was able to establish Irish colonies there. Later, in 519, St. Brendan the Navigator left Ireland in a similar craft on a five-year voyage. Legend tells that he reached Iceland, and even North America.

The skin umiak of the Eskimos was used for whale hunting, but as this gradually ceased, it became an all-purpose craft, sometimes used for hunting but more often for carrying families and goods to new homes when necessary.

The frame was very much the same as one of a conventional carvel-built boat, except that it was fastened with skin thongs and was built of driftwood. It was covered with some fifteen to twenty sealskins, sewn into sections by Eskimo women, then stretched and secured inboard by thongs to the stringers

The Irish curragh

15

beneath the gunwales. The umiak was approximately thirty feet long with a beam of five to six feet. The mast carried a lug-type sail of reindeer skin (in later years blue or white cotton drill was used). The boat carried several pairs of oars, a long steering oar and a bailer. The umiak carried specialized equipment of carved and ornamented walrus ivory—such as boat fittings, harpoon rests, lance toggles, snow and ice beaters for clearing the boat, clothing and strings of good-luck charms.

Norse longships
The Norwegian Vikings jealously claimed the name 'North-men' for themselves, but ethnically the term is much broader. It embraces all the Scandinavian peoples, the Saxons, Jutes and Angles, the Slavonic Wends of the Baltic coast, the Norse settlers of Iceland, the Germanic Franks, the Finns and Russians, the Enskirmenn or English, the Irskirmenn or Irish and many others. Thus, as in the Southern Hemisphere, the ship development of the North was a multi-racial affair. The northern seamen, faced with the fury of winter winds and waves and racing tides unknown in the Mediterranean, built their ships accordingly. Even today the Norse longship is regarded by experts as the most seaworthy type of basic sailing vessel ever evolved.

In 1939 the remains of a Saxon longship were unearthed at Sutton Hoo, near Woodbridge, England. Although no wood

The Sutton Hoo Ship,
length 84ft., beam 14ft.

The Gokstad Ship, built about a thousand years ago; length 77ft., beam 17ft. Above it is the *Hugin*, a 20th-century version of a Viking snekja.

was found, the dimensions of the Sutton Hoo Ship could be calculated from the position of the iron nails still remaining. It was considered the most important ship find in the northern hemisphere because of the splendid treasures it contained. Chief of these (now on display in the British Museum) was a massive sword with a solid gold jewel-encrusted hilt and a unique fibula of gold, which indicated that this may have been the memorial of Aethelhere, a Saxon king of East Anglia.

Nevertheless, the discovery in 1880 of the twenty-ton, oak-built Gokstad Ship near Sandjefiord, Norway, was of equally great significance. For, where the Sutton Hoo Ship had rotted completely, the Gokstad Ship had been buried in blue clay which had preserved it almost intact for a thousand years. Built approximately three centuries after the Sutton Hoo Ship, the Gokstad Ship had a sepulchral chamber containing a carved wooden bier on which lay the remains of a Norse sea warrior with a massive axe, iron plates and buckles of his war harness, a large chest that served as the ship's armory, and items of wood and iron ship chandlery. Along each bulwark of the ship were thirty-two wooden shields, alternately colored black and yellow, while each oar-port was sealed with a wooden disc or deadlight to keep the water out when the ship was heeling under sail.

A replica very similar to the Gokstad Ship can be seen at Pegwell Bay near Ramsgate, England. This ship, the *Hugin*, was built of oak at Frederikssund near Copenhagen, and in 1949, with a crew of fifty-three men dressed as Vikings, she crossed from Esbjerg to the Kent coast in two weeks. The 'Vikings' brought gifts of silver and amber to commemorate their ancestors. The *Hugin*, built from records at Greenwich and Copenhagen, was an average-sized Viking ship known as a snekja or 'snake', seventy-one feet overall with a beam of eighteen feet, which could carry up to 150 men. The biggest longships, known collectively as *herskips*—meaning 'hosts of war'—and individually as *drekis,* or 'dragons', were infinitely more formidable in size and crew. The saga of King Olaf Trygvasson who ruled Norway a thousand years ago, tells of such a ship—the *Ormrinn Langi* or 'Long Serpent': 'King Olaf had a large ship built at Hladhamrar. It was 180 feet long with a beam exceeding thirty-eight feet and with stem- and stern-posts rising fifteen feet above the water. Thorberg Skarfhogg was the stemsmith (shipwright). Besides being long and broad, the ship had high bulwarks and massive timbers and all men said that they had never seen such a fine or large longship. Early one morning the King and Thorberg went to look at the ship and found great cuts in both bulwarks. The King was greatly angered by what he saw and said that if he knew the man who had spoiled the ship then that man should die, but not easily. He promised that the man who told him of the culprit's name should have a great reward. Then said Thorberg: "I can tell you, king, who did this thing." "Then tell it!" said the King. "I have done it," said Thorberg. "Then," said the King, "Thou shalt repair it so that it is as good as before—or lose thy life!" Then Thorberg took his axe and shaped one side of the ship so that the cuts had disappeared, and everyone said that the ship was even better on that side that it was before. Then the King asked Thorberg to do the same on the other side, and when it was done he thanked him well.'

The *Long Serpent* was said to have been the finest and costliest longship ever built in Norway and had a total complement of 700 men. The biggest longship known in history was Knut (King Canute) the Great's *Great Dragon*. It was 300 feet overall, manned by 120 oarsmen and carried a total complement of approximately one thousand. *Leidangr* was a highly organized system of ship levy which enabled the Norsemen to assemble the largest fleets of any maritime people. The two largest of these fleets, totaling from 5,000 to 6,000 longships, were engaged in the Battle of Bravoll, Eastern Gautland, in A.D. 700.

The Oseberg Ship, a fine example of a Viking longship.

Norse naval tactics—and their ships—were highly developed. For example, they used a type of 'armored cruiser' known as a jarnbardi. This was a large, reinforced longship armored above the water line with iron plates and carrying a deadly iron-spiked skegg or 'beard' on the bow, for ramming. Such a formidable and unconventional vessel, commanded by Eric Jarl, son of Hakon Jarl who ruled Norway A.D. 965–995, did great execution at the bloody battles of Swold and Jomsvikings.

The Norsemen used as many as 3,000 ships, and supply vessels were essential: capacious vistabrydings (ships of burden) carried food, livestock, weapons and ammuniton, and smiths and forges for repair work at sea. The hepiskuta or 'running ship' carried dispatches. The cargo ship (kaup skip) was greater in beam and depth than the longship, carried no shields on its rails, lacked the 'war girdle' (a massive hawser used to strengthen the hulls of warships) and had no pennants or dragons' heads. Such a ship is described in Egil's Saga:

'Thorolf had a large seagoing ship which was most carefully built and painted all over above the water line. It had a sail of red and blue stripes and all the rigging was very elaborate. This ship Thorolf made ready and ordered his menservants to go with it. He put on board dried fish, skins, tallow and furs from the mountains—all of great value. Thorolf set the ship westward to buy woollen cloth and other goods he needed. They went southward and then out to sea. When they arrived

The Norse kaup skip, a large, seagoing cargo vessel

The Kalmar Boat, length 36ft., beam 15ft.

in England they found a good market, loaded the ship with wheat, honey, wines and cloth and returned in the autumn with fair winds'.

The Norsemen traded to all ports of Western Europe and in the Mediterranean and Adriatic Seas; they also sailed to the Black Sea and penetrated by caravan to the heart of Russia.

By the Middle Ages, however, the magnificent longships of the Northmen had lost their striking lines and had come more and more to resemble the Mediterranean 'round ship'. A good example of this type of vessel is the thirteenth-century Kalmar Boat, discovered with many other sunken vessels dating to the seventeenth century in the bay of Kalmar Castle, Sweden, when it was drained between 1932 and 1934.

The oak, clinker-built hull of the Kalmar Boat, when

compared to the earlier longships, is disproportionately broad, having a beam of fifteen feet to an overall length of thirty-six feet. This short, rigid, stoutly beamed vessel, decked-in fore-and-aft was driven by a mainsail of 270 square feet, on a sturdy mast stepped amidships.

The cog, caravel and carrack

The stern-mounted rudder probably first appeared in the twelfth century (one is carved on the font of Winchester Cathedral). By the early 1200's European ships had changed radically. Forecastles and aftercastles were being built at bow and stern. The mainmast now had a topcastle—forerunner of the fighting tops of the massive 'wooden-walls'—from which iron bars and quicklime were hurled. Thwartship beams now protruded through the planking, the ends secured

A 14th-century cog, length 90ft., beam 24ft.

by strong wooden pegs. For the first time in history the square mainsail had reef points for shortening sail in heavy weather.

During the thirteenth century the cog appeared, a single-masted, sweep-propelled vessel some ninety feet long, with a ten-foot draught. It was strong, clumsy and completely decked-in. The mast was equipped with ratlines secured to the shrouds, to enable the crew to reach the topcastle.

The carrack, which followed the cog, had two to four masts and a capacity of 200 to 600 tons—a rating based on the tuns of wine carried. It was distinguished by its overhanging fore-castle and aftercastle and the 'bonaventure' mast stepped aft of the mizzenmast. A square spritsail on the bowsprit was used to steady the ship's head; fore- and mainmasts were square-rigged, the mizzenmast and bonaventure lateen-rigged.

The carrack reached its peak in Genoa and Venice. History's most famous carrack was Columbus's *Santa Maria*: she was approximately eighty feet overall, with a beam of some twenty-six feet and driven by some 3,500 square feet of canvas.

The carrack, length 80–100ft., beam 25–35ft.

A Portuguese caravel

The caravel, of Portuguese origin, was a two- or three-masted, shallow-draught vessel, swifter and more graceful than the carrack, with two distinct sail rigs. The *caravela latina* was lateen-rigged on all masts; the *caravela redonda* was fully square-rigged or both square- and lateen-rigged.

Used largely for coastal work, caravels played an important part in maritime history, for Henry the Navigator, of Portugal, used them at the beginning of the fifteenth century to open up the trade routes to India. *Santa Clara* (called *Niña* after her captain Juan Niño), which accompanied the *Santa Maria* to America, was about sixty tons, seventy feet overall, with a twenty-four-foot beam and a draught of six feet. She started as a *caravela latina,* but Columbus found this rig unsuitable for the existing winds and converted her to a *caravela redonda*

24

in the Canary Islands. This was done by stepping the raking mainmast well forward in a vertical position and strengthening it by means of a forestay to a bowsprit. The long lateen yards were cut down to square-rigged yards and the suit of lateen sails recut to fit them.

By the end of the fifteenth century ships were reaching out into the Atlantic. The Mediterranean oared galley was no match for this stormy ocean, and it lacked carrying capacity. Thus the galleasse, a type of oared frigate, came into existence. They carried the first cannon to fire *through* gunports instead of over them (*en barbette*). The galleasse vanished in the eighteenth century, a period when it resembled a gracefully sheered, topsail rigged ketch.

The galleasse, a type of oared frigate; a number of these ships sailed with the Armada.

25

TRADITIONAL SAILING CRAFT

Many kinds of sailing vessels originated in comparatively
early times and have survived, in non-industrial civilizations,
to perform useful work well into the twentieth century.

Nile gaiassa

Egypt

Boatbuilders on the Nile still lack suitable timber. Sunt and sycamore grow only in short lengths, and although hard they are brittle and difficult to work. Craft are made of planks four to six feet long which are joined together, giving the vessels an inherent weakness; built by 'rule of thumb', they are rough and ungainly.

The two- and three-masted, lateen-rigged gaiassa is a maid of all work. Gaiassas do not sail against the wind, they only sail with it, and then drift back with the current.

The Dongola markab, found on the Dongola Reach of the Nile, is like the gaiassa but with one well-stayed mast amidships. The sail is slung obliquely from the masthead and has two yards, one at the head and one at the foot of the sail. It is shallow-draught all-purpose vessel, with a powerful rudder.

The nuggar, found in the vicinity of Omdurman, is a crudely built, shallow-draught vessel, undecked, broad in the beam and carrying a single mast stepped amidships. It is propelled by

Dongola markab

Nile nuggar

27

a sail almost identical to that of the markab. The nuggar is most frequently used as a ferry boat, and smaller nuggars may serve as tenders to the larger ones. The largest type of nuggar is approximately sixty-two feet overall, has a crew of six to eight men, and carries cargoes of between forty and fifty tons.

The Arabs

The Arabs, and particularly the Saracens, were a virile

The two-masted, lateen-rigged baghla, an Arab ship of striking appearance

The fast, shallow-draught zaruk

and fearless people who, after encountering the mariners of Phoenicia and Greece, quickly grasped the significance of naval power and sea trade.

Today the Arabs have their own distinctive types of sailing vessels known collectively by Europeans, but not by the Arabs, as dhows.

Most impressive of all the Arabs' sailing ships is the shapely and seaworthy baghla, a two-masted, lateen-rigged vessel which incorporates many innovations of both hemispheres. The lofty, ornately carved and decorated poop is similar to that of a fifteenth-century caravel while the massive rudder is housed in a rudder trunk after the manner of the old East Indiamen. Also reminiscent of the caravel is the carvel-built hull of the baghla, on which the planks are laid edge to edge instead of overlapping.

The sleekly sinister zaruk, a fast, shallow-draught, single-masted, lateen-rigged vessel used for the coastal trade in the Gulf of Aden, the Persian Gulf and the Red Sea, is of unusual design which, unlike that of the baghla, shows no European

The sambuk, a two-masted, lateen-rigged vessel from the Red Sea.

influence. The bow rakes sharply forward and the narrow rudder extends well below the keel and is operated by an unusual arrangement of blocks and tackles. Because of its speed, handiness and the shallow draught which permitted it to elude capture by slipping across shoals and sandbanks, the zaruk was favored up to comparatively recent times by slavers, gun-runners and smugglers, especially ivory smugglers. Also used by pearl-diving communities, the zaruk is sometimes known as the garookuh.

The graceful, carvel-built, two-masted, lateen-rigged sambuk of the Red Sea, like the baghla, shows definite early-

European influence in its forward-raking masts and built-up poop deck, the quarters of which are decorated with gaily painted lozenges, arcades and bands, after the manner of an Elizabethan galleon.

The single-masted, lateen-rigged badan, most frequently seen in the waters around Aden, like the zaruk, was frequently used for all manner of nefarious schemes because of its speed, ease of handling and shallow draught. This vessel has the same distinctive rudder and steering gear as the zaruk while the stempiece is almost straight, lacking the extreme rake that is characteristic of the zaruk.

Both zaruk and badan, unlike the larger, square-sterned baghla, have sharp sterns, a feature that makes both types of vessel particularly suitable for handling in heavy following seas or heavy surf.

The badan, most commonly found near Aden, is a coastal ship favored by smugglers grateful for her speed and ease of handling.

Mediterranean craft

The Mediterranean and Aegean seas were enhanced up to thirty or forty years ago by a multitude of unusually rigged and gaily adorned sailing vessels, bearing equally colorful names. These vessels, which have unfortunately vanished almost without trace before the onset of marine engines and politics, illustrate the incorporation of both Mediterranean and Northern European aspects of ship design and sail plan.

Among the most graceful of these vanished ships was the two-masted Venetian rascona. Equipped with a single steering oar on the starboard quarter of the long and graceful hull, propelled by two European-type lugsails adorned with gay devices and with a large deck-cabin aft, the rascona was a combination of the basic Mediterranean round-ship and northern longship, with the emphasis on the latter.

The Genoese vinco was one of the most spectacular of all the

Venetian rascona

Genoese vinco

traditional-type Mediterranean sailing vessels. The built-up stern and sweep of the hull were similar to those of the Algerian chebek, while the sail plan and mast rig was a distinct combination of Mediterranean and Northern European concepts. The foremast carried three square sails and yards together with an outer jib, inner jib and foresail stayed to a long bowsprit, complete with 'dolphin striker', after the manner of northern ships. The mainmast and mizzen, on the other hand, carried the traditional lateen sails of the Mediterranean. The mizzen sail was controlled from a 'bumpkin' or short spar extending over the stern.

Maltese sperona

33

Greek scapho

The single-masted, lateen-rigged Maltese sperona has an unusual projection of the bow reminiscent of the ram of the Greek war galleys, while the high rail around the deck probably evolved from the deck screens of plaited osiers used by the early Greek trading ships to protect their cargoes. European influence shows in the centrally mounted rudder, long bowsprit and large triangular foresail.

The Greek scapho was an unusual vessel in that its general appearance was almost completely Northern European. The hull was similar in shape to the open fishing dories used on the coast of North America and was clinker-built (i.e., with overlapping planks). The huge, gaff-rigged mainsail was further reinforced by a long diagonal spar or sprit, after the manner of the Thames sailing barges—that were known as 'spritties'. The only traditional Mediterranean feature of this somewhat ungainly looking vessel is the canvas 'dodger' or screen laced to the deck rails.

The Greek sacoleva was an even more striking combination of northern and southern innovations than the scapho. It was one of those traditional Mediterranean craft about which relatively little is known. The vertical mainmast carried a

34

gaff-rigged mainsail. Above the mainsail was a yard which carried a square sail. The vertical mizzenmast carried a lateen sail which was controlled from a 'bumpkin'. At first glance the sacoleva could be taken for a European topsail schooner until closer examination shows the traditional Mediterranean 'round-ship' hull, adapted for greater cargo capacity. An unusual feature is that both masts are almost of the same length, whereas the topsail schooner has a foremast which is much shorter than the mainmast. Finally, where the topsail schooner carries a gaff mainsail and a gaff maintopsail, the sacoleva is rigged with a lateen sail only on the after mast.

The Turkish tchektirme (overleaf) is another interesting combination of Mediterranean and Northern European ship design. The hull was carvel-built, the planks laid edge to edge, in the traditional Mediterranean style; but the sprit-rigged mainsail, foresail, inner jib, outer jib and long, canted bowsprit gave the tchektirme a striking similarity to a nineteenth-century North Sea cutter-rigged sailing trawler.

Greek sacoleva

The single-masted Turkish mahovna, or sailing barge, carried a large lateen sail laced to a long, counterweighted yard which was slung to a stump mast.

The shape and sheer of the bow are distinctly Egyptian in appearance, being almost identical to the bow of the large, lateen-rigged Nile boom. The long bowsprit holding the foresail and jib, on the other hand, gives the forepart of the mahovna a definitely European look. It is unforunate that the Turks appear to have kept no record of the construction or functions of their earlier, more humble types of traditional sailing craft, though, like the billyboy, hoy and other quaintly named traditional types of English sailing craft, they seem to have been maritime 'maids of all work'.

Powered vessels have mostly displaced these picturesque and exotically named craft although a few can be found scattered along the ports of the Mediterranean and Aegean Seas. But, like the tan-sailed trawlers and drifters that once thronged the east coast fishing ports of England, they have been shorn of their sails and reduced to stump masts and diesel or gasoline engines.

The single-masted Turkish tchektirme, with its sprit-rigged mainsail, foresail and two jibs.

The mahovna, a single-masted Turkish sailing barge.

Spanish and Portuguese vessels

The single-masted, lateen-rigged Spanish tartane (overleaf) is another example of a basically Mediterranean-type vessel incorporating innovations from Northern Europe. For, while the stem extending well above the bow follows a Greek concept, the triangular jib and bowsprit indicate European influence.

The two-masted, lateen-rigged Spanish felucca bore a striking resemblance to the Algerian Corsairs' chebek, with its forward-raking mainmast, extended stempiece, its 'lute' or overhanging stern, long bowsprit and big foresail. Indeed, it is likely that the Spaniards were strongly influenced by the chebek's speed, seaworthiness and graceful lines. The felucca of later times is a long, double-ended, or transom-sterned, open boat, carrying a single forward-raking mast and the traditional lateen, which is an outstanding example of Mediterranean sail development. Originally a conventional square lug-type sail, the lateen had its leading or weather edge

A Portuguese
moliceiro

—known as the *luff*—greatly reduced, and the yard thus set at
an angle. The reason for this modification was that while the
original type of sail was satisfactory in light airs, it caused the
felucca to bury its bow in the sudden fierce winds of the
Mediterranean.

Like the colorful traditional sailing vessels of the Mediterranean, the Spanish tartane and the felucca have now disappeared in the wake of the marine engine, hastened by the
Spanish government's disapproving attitude toward the
continuation of traditional wooden sailing vessels.

Typically Mediterranean in rig and form, except for the
clinker-built hull, was the two-masted, lateen-rigged Portuguese Tagus frigata which, as its name suggests, originated on
the River Tagus. Characteristic of this sailing vessel were the
stump masts of equal length; the mizzenmast raking slightly
aft; the extended and ornately decorated stem- and stern-
pieces, and the decorative panels on the bow.

A two-masted
Spanish felucca.

The tartane, also
a traditional
Spanish vessel.

The Tagus frigata,
a Portuguese vessel built
in the Mediterranean
tradition.

51620L

A Portuguese
wine boat

The Douro wine boat, which carried port down the River Douro to Oporto for maturing, was an extremely primitive craft, yet well designed for its particular function. The hull — distinctly Egyptian in form with a long upward-curving bow and stern (see gaiassa, page 26) — was broad-beamed and of shallow draught, built with the minimum of cross beams in order to facilitate the stowing of wine casks. The Nilotic appearance of this craft was increased by the huge, loose-bellied square sail set on a mast stepped slightly aft, and the tower-like wooden platform from which the boat was steered around the sharp bends of the Douro by means of a ponderous sweep, or oar (projecting to the right of the picture).

The strange looking Portuguese muletta, used for both drift-net (surface fishing) and trawling (bottom fishing) was, despite its appearance, well designed for its function. The large lateen sail, set on a forward-raking mast and supplemented by a primitive form of double spinnaker, gave the vessel forward movement. The muletta is one of the most interesting sailing vessels in existence, for it incorporates features of the ships of three maritime peoples far removed in place and time: the iron spiked bow was identical to the 'skegg' or 'beard' of a type of armored Norse longship known as a jarnbardi; the gaily painted *oculi* on the bow were traditionally Mediterranean, and the tub-shaped hull and leeboards were reminiscent of a nineteenth-century Dutch hektjalk.

The Portuguese muletta, a
fishing craft of unusual rig.
Note the *oculus* on the bow.

41

Two vessels of
the Ganges: the
patile (*above*)
and the palla.

India

The Ganges patile, a large single-masted, lugsail-rigged cargo vessel, is unusual in that it is probably the only clinker-built boat to be found on the River Ganges. An unusual feature, to Western eyes, is the palm-thatched deckhouse extending almost the entire length of the vessel and mounted by a bamboo catwalk, from the after end of which the patile is steered by means of a long-loomed, balanced rudder. The massive blade of this powerful rudder extends well forward of the rudder stock, thus providing the extra control needed when the vessel is heavily laden. The patile is sometimes adorned with *oculi* on the bow.

The single-masted, lugsail-rigged palla, or pulwa, and the mala pansi have upward-curving bows and sterns in the Egyptian manner and rudders mounted on the port quarter. The hulls of both are carvel-built, and the mast of the mala pansi is stepped in a tall tabernacle which permits it to be lowered aft when the wind fails and paddles must be used. Both craft have the conventional palm-thatched cabin. They are used to ferry market produce across the Ganges.

The mala pansi, one of the smallest of the Ganges sailing craft.

An unconventional but highly efficient craft is the carvel-built balance-board fishing boat of the Palk Strait, between India and Ceylon. Instead of depending on the more usual type of outrigger (see page 57), it has a long plank of heavy palmyra wood which is lashed athwartships and secured each side by a shroud from the mast. In fresh winds the balance-board is run out on the weather side of the boat and given additional support by the lee shroud, which is shifted to the weather side of the board to serve also as a lifeline.

These balance-board boats are lugsail-rigged on one to three masts and they are of shallow draught, with no keel. This shallow draught enables them to feel their way along the maze of shallow, narrow channels amid the offshore mud banks, and

The spectacular kola maram, also known as the 'flying-fish' catamaran.

A lugsail-rigged balance-
board fishing boat from
the Palk Strait.

combines with their length and large sail area to make them the
swiftest of the traditional Indian sailing craft. They are
equipped with a narrow leeboard to counteract the lack of
keel and have two thin steering oars manipulated by the feet
of the helmsman, who squats on a small deck in the stern.

The most spectacular of all the 'catamarans' (Indian
kattumaran = tied logs) is the big, seven-log kola maram or
'flying-fish catamaran' of the Coromandel Coast. It consists of
seven big logs securely lashed together, narrowed at the
bow and having five upward-curving stempieces, which
help the craft to skim at speed in pursuit of flying fish. Again,
leeboards are lowered to counteract the lack of keel. The crew
are forced to spend long periods aboard to make the most of
the short fishing season.

Southeast Asia

From the beginning of history the dense jungles of Burma and Thailand have made the Irawadi, Salween and Mekong Rivers the only means of transport over vast tracts of land. Because of this the native boats and vessels have developed through the centuries from the first crude dugout canoes to large, picturesque and highly specialized sailing craft which clearly retain the basic structure of their primitive prototypes.

The hull of the Irawadi rice boat still has the form of the dugout canoe in the underpart, which is built by steaming the frame and then stretching it to the required beam when flexible. The high bulwarks, lofty and ornately carved poop, massive and powerful rudder shipped on the port quarter, the huge, swag-bellied sails, the long, palm-thatched deckhouse and the outboard galleries from which the vessel is poled when necessary—all are innovations of the passing centuries. Magnificent carving on the poop forms floral scrolls incorporat-

The picturesque
Irawadi rice boat

46

ing the flowers and creepers of the jungle.

The small rua chalom, frequently seen on the waters around Thailand, is a busy 'maid-of-all-work,' cargo boat. Characteristic of this single-masted lugsailed boat, with its bamboo-roofed deckhouse and gracefully sheered stem- and sternposts, are the narrow-bladed rudders, one on each quarter, giving the rua chalom the likeness of an early Mediterranean trading vessel.

The flat-bottomed Thai twako, with its battened lugsails, raking foremast and brightly painted hull adorned with *oculi* on the bow is, to all intents and purposes, a Chinese junk. Unlike the junk, however, the twako is steered by a rudder shipped conventionally to the sternpost, instead of the junk-type rudder which passes through a rudder trunk in the poop. The ghe ca vom (overleaf), a long, narrow riverboat of Vietnam has a distinctly Egyptian appearance, strengthened by the short lengths of timber of the hull. The single mast, which is stepped well forward, carries an unusual sail, a combination of Oriental lugsail and Occidental gaff sail. A small bamboo deckhouse shelters the crew, and the

The rua chalom

The twako

47

The ghe ca vom, a narrow riverboat from Vietnam.

rudder, mounted on the sternpost, curves gracefully beneath the hull, thus giving greater purchase and control.

The ghe luoi rung is a mixture of East and West. This picturesque boat has a shallow, spoon-shaped, gaily painted, carvel-built hull, bearing a large *oculus* on each bow—all features which recall the model funeral ships found in Egyptian tombs. But the three upright masts are stayed, European fashion, by dead-eyes secured to chain-plates, and the mainmast is powerfully stayed to a bow bearing a miniature figurehead. Most astonishing of all is the sail plan, known as the Gunter rig—once esteemed in the British Royal Navy for its smart appearance and ease of handling. The rudder is like that of the ghe ca vom. The *oculus* symbolized the watchful and protective eye of the ancient Egyptian god Horus. The Stone Age mariners of Crete also adopted this symbol to depict the eyes of their ancient mother-goddess Rhea, protectress of sailors (among other things). Eventually the *oculi* were adopted by the Phoenicians, the Greeks, the Romans and even by the Portuguese, whose boats still bear them. The belief in the benign and watchful ship deity, eternally alert for dangers seen through the symbolic eyes, spread to Africa and Asia: the vessels of Zanzibar have *oculi* on bow and stern; the Chinese adopted three forms, 'The Dragon's Eye', 'The Tadpole Eye' and 'The Phoenix Eye'.

This far-reaching cult has become very complex. If the crew are Hindu or Buddhist their craft will most likely be adorned with *oculi*. Islam, however, forbids the practice.

The ghe luoi rung, its bow adorned with *oculi*. Sailors still speak of the forepart as the 'eyes' of a ship.

China

The junk—perhaps the oldest traditional type of sailing vessel in existence—has largely retained its original shape. The hull has a short bow and stern and no keel; it probably developed from a primitive form of double canoe.

The Hoangho Ch' uan, or Yellow River junk, was the simplest in form and has been called 'a floating packing crate'. Built of iron-clamped planks of Tung Liu Mu wood, it was divided into three more or less watertight compartments and had a cargo capacity of about twenty tons.

The Pechili trading junk, found near Singapore until 1910, with its crew of twenty to thirty men, is regarded as the oldest type of Chinese sea-junk. This vessel—flat-bottomed to permit running aground on sandbanks without damage—was of impressive dimensions: 140 to 180 feet overall, with a beam of 20 to 30 feet and a cargo capacity of up to 400 tons.

The Pechili trader, built in Shanghai to trade between Yinghow, Shanghai and the other ports of Kiangsi and Chekiang, was unique in the stepping of its masts. The foremast was stepped outboard on the port side; the two mainmasts and mizzen were stepped in line. Well aft on the port side, an

The Hoangho Ch'uan or Yellow River junk, additionally known as a 'floating packing crate' and capable of carrying cargoes of up to 20 tons.

The Pechili trading junk

auxiliary mizzen was stepped just clear of the tiller and used to bring the ship about when tacking.

In addition to the large lugsails, a staysail was frequently set between the two mainmasts and — most unusual in a junk — a large topsail was set to give greater way to the unwieldy vessel in light airs. A long deckhouse aft provided shelter for the crew, while an extended 'lute-stern' type of afterdeck provided working space for the handling of the mizzen sails. Decorations were few.

51

The three-masted, lugsail-rigged Foochow pole junk was once a common sight off the coast of China, with its deck cargo of poles. It was a lumbering vessel with a cargo capacity of 200 to 400 tons, and was generally reinforced with thin iron plating imported from British scrap merchants: it was not unusual to see a junk bearing an advertisement for 'Wright's Coal Tar Soap'.

The sails were the conventional battened lugsail of heavy white or brown canvas; decoration varied according to the home port. The crew of twenty to thirty men lived aft in a big deckhouse under the protection of the ship's deity, or joss.

Their massive hardwood frames, divided into watertight thwartship compartments every eight feet, and fore-and-aft compartments every four feet, made these cumbersome craft

The Foochow pole junk

The Chinese lorcha, first built in Macao in 1843.

eminently seaworthy; the pole junk *Keying,* commanded by Captain Kellet, sailed from Hong Kong via the Cape of Good Hope to London in 1848. In 1908 the *Whangho* sailed from Hong Kong to Sydney, and in 1912 the *Ningpo* made a voyage from Shanghai to San Francisco.

The Chinese lorcha was an unusual vessel—a hybrid, like the polacca-chebek. The first lorchas were built by the Portuguese at Macao in 1843 to fight the pirates who swarmed the China seas and rivers. They had Chinese sail rigs and flat-bottomed westernized hulls built of teak and camphor wood. In 1847, seven lorchas cleaned out the pirate nests of the Ningpo area. After this the lorchas were of no further use to the Portuguese, who sold them. Thus these specialized vessels—later copied by the Chinese—fell into the hands of gunrunners and smugglers. Just before the breed declined, a Chinese lorcha, the *Arrow,* was instrumental in sparking off the Sino-British War of 1857–60. Until about 1865 lorchas were easily identified by their paintwork: rusty-red, with a bright yellow poop and forecastle and a white deckhouse.

Japan and Formosa

It is an astonishing anomaly to find that the Japanese—a true maritime people—should have but one type of junk and that of poor design and performance.

It was a beamy, heavily built, lugsail-rigged vessel, with two or three masts. It had, however, an inherent and dangerous defect: the open well of the stern, built to permit the raising and lowering of the rudder, rendered the vessel very liable to be pooped, that is, swamped by a wave breaking over the stern. Most surprising of all, the side galleries and artemon-like foremast were almost identical to those of the early Roman corn ships.

The heavy surf of the east coast of Formosa has caused the evolution of a type of sailing raft which is considered to be the most advanced of this class of sailing transport. The Taiwan raft is built of large bamboos, curving upward at each side and at the bow. The mast is a large stem of bamboo, and the matting sail is the traditional type of Chinese sail, supported by

Japanese junk

The Taiwan raft,
built to weather the
heavy surf off the
east coast of
Formosa.

cross battens. To prevent the craft making leeway when under
sail the crew push narrow boards down between the bamboo
stems of the hull.

This was a Chinese innovation from which the drop-keel or
center-board has been developed. In the center of the raft is a
large wooden tub with a plank seat on which passengers sit to
keep their feet dry. In addition to the sail, the raft is equipped
with six large, self-feathering oars which are known as
'yulohs'.

The self-feathering action of the yulohs is obtained by the
blade of the oar being at a slight angle to the loom or handle.
This obviates the necessity of the oarsman turning the blade
of his oar when it leaves the water.

Indonesia

In times past, the two-masted flying-prau, or prahu, of Java, which originated in Malaya, was a sight all voyagers in the Java Sea feared: she carried heavy swivel guns fore and aft and was usually a pirate ship.

The flying-prau was fifty feet long and had a fourteen-foot beam. She was a hybrid, for her high poop and long bowsprit, with conventional triangular jib, were Western innovations; while the two steering oars (one on each quarter), the outboard galleries and the peculiar curve of the masthead showed Mediterranean influence. The bipod mast and the frameless, teak-planked hull supported by cross-beams, inserted after the hull was built, are identical to those of traditional early Egyptian craft.

The sail plan of the flying-prau altered little over the centuries, as illustrated by the ship carvings of Boro-Badur, Java, which were executed nearly a thousand years ago. A characteristic of this rakish craft was the primitive but effective way in which the crew kept their food from rats and other vermin that inevitably haunted the prau: they just slung their rations from the mast in a large earthenware pot.

The prau bedang, from Madura, near Java, is a long, two-masted craft with double outriggers. Steered by a single oar, the prau bedang is higher in the stern than the bow, which

The flying-prau, or prahu, from Java.

56

The prau bedang from Madura, equipped with double outriggers.

projects forward in the form of a ram. The mast plan resembles that of a two-masted schooner, with the mainmast stepped near the stern and the shorter foremast stepped well forward. The triangular sails, with the head laced to a yard and the foot laced to a boom, appear to be a hybrid form of lug-lateen.

In complete contrast to the long prau bedang, the two-masted, carvel-built, cargo carrying prau mayang is of the 'round-ship' form. Steered by an oar from the port quarter, this craft carries a large lug-lateen type of sail on the main-mast, which is stepped well forward. The long bowsprit and triangular fore-staysail show marked Western influence. A large cabin, open at the stern, shelters crew and cargo.

The prau mayang, a cargo
vessel built on
'round-ship' lines.

57

The caracor, a double outrigger indigenous to the waters of New Guinea, the Celebes, Borneo and Java, has stem- and sternposts extended somewhat in the manner of a Norse longship. The tripod mast carries a large lug-lateen type of sail, the head laced to a long yard and the foot to a long boom. The craft is steered by an oar shipped on the port quarter. Because of its speed and general handiness the caracor was used by the Dutch as a patrol boat until comparatively recently.

Like the flying-prau of Java, the tripod-masted Moro outrigger boat of the Sulu Sea was always given a wide berth, for it was frequently manned by Moro headhunters. The hull of this primitive but dangerous craft consisted of a simple dugout canoe balanced by a single heavy outrigger to port. The tripod mast carried a very large sail of the lug-lateen type, which gave the outrigger tremendous speed when it was sailing with a fair wind.

The double-outrigger caracor, a native Indonesian craft.

The primitive Moro outrigger, often manned by head-hunters.

The South Pacific

The dugout canoe is the most primitive and widespread of all forms of water transport, being used by prehistoric man all over the world. In Britain, for example, two dugout canoes were found when the Ribble Docks were being dug at Preston. These dugout canoes were suitable logs, hollowed out by fire or stone axes; in the South Pacific axes made from the hard shell of the tridacna, or giant clam, were used.

The New Guinea lakatoi (overleaf) consists of three or more large dugout canoes formed into a single craft by passing stout beams through them. A solid bamboo platform is then lashed to the completed hull, while two masts—stepped close together amidships—are rigged with odd sails which are shaped like the claws of a giant lobster.

These unusual craft—which show neither oriental nor occidental influence—are approximately sixty feet overall, with a beam of fifty feet; thus the lakatoi resembles a sailing raft rather than a true boat. It is stable but unwieldy, requiring three cumbersome paddles, pivoted at the stern, to steer it. Principally used by the Papuans of Port Moresby for trading and for ceremonial races, the craft were decorated with tassels and garlands of leaves and carried a troupe of dancing girls at the fore end. The lakatoi was large enough to carry up to thirty people on a long coastal voyage.

The Tongan calie was a double canoe, one canoe shorter than the other, and was used for fishing and carrying goods, passengers and raiding parties. It consisted of two canoes lashed together by large beams which supported a platform holding the mast and deckhouse. Extra free-board was achieved by raising the sides of the canoes by means of planks sewn on with palm-fiber twine. The foreward-raking

A triple-hulled, two-masted New
Guinea lakatoi, with
claw-shaped sails.

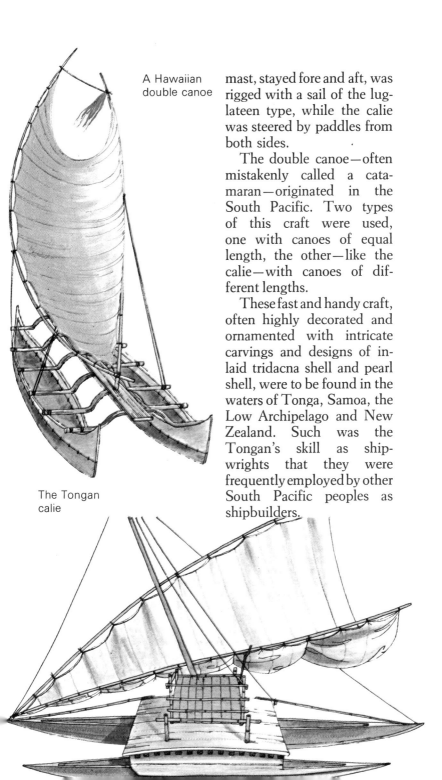

A Hawaiian double canoe

mast, stayed fore and aft, was rigged with a sail of the lug-lateen type, while the calie was steered by paddles from both sides.

The double canoe—often mistakenly called a cata-maran—originated in the South Pacific. Two types of this craft were used, one with canoes of equal length, the other—like the calie—with canoes of different lengths.

These fast and handy craft, often highly decorated and ornamented with intricate carvings and designs of in-laid tridacna shell and pearl shell, were to be found in the waters of Tonga, Samoa, the Low Archipelago and New Zealand. Such was the Tongan's skill as ship-wrights that they were frequently employed by other South Pacific peoples as shipbuilders.

The Tongan calie

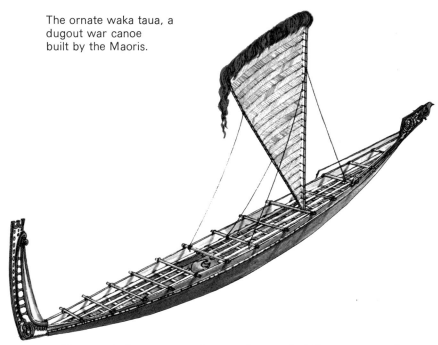

The ornate waka taua, a
dugout war canoe
built by the Maoris.

For a period covering a thousand years the Maoris, a mixed
Polynesian and Melanesian people, set out on great transpacific migrations to New Zealand. The type of vessel they
used was an enormous double canoe called a tainui. They were
over seventy feet long and were driven on their formidable
voyages by means of two claw-shaped sails, similar to those of
the lakatoi, supported on lofty bipod masts. On the massive
cross-beams which joined the two huge canoes of the hull, a
stout platform was built to hold a large cabin, which was the
accommodation of the chief and his men, while the women-
folk lived in one of the canoes. The food supplies for the
migrants were carried in deep holds. The tainui was remarkable for the huge, blade-shaped decorations of the stern which
were twenty feet high and ornamented with the traditional
spiral motif of the Maoris. Like the Tongan calie, the Maori
tainui was given additional free-board by means of extra
planking sewn on with palm-fiber twine.

When the sea-weary Maoris reached New Zealand, they
were quick to utilize the huge Kauri pine trees to build their

magnificent war canoe, the waka taua, the most ornate of all the traditional craft of the Pacific Ocean. Propelled both by paddles and by a sail in the form of an inverted triangle, the waka taua was a single dugout canoe, seventy feet long and with a beam of only five feet—dimensions which gave this handsome craft tremendous speed.

Like the tainui, the waka taua carried a tall, blade-shaped decoration at the stern, while the ornately carved bow bore the figure of a fearsome mythical creature called the 'Manaia'—its tongue protruding in the traditional war grimace of the fierce Maori warriors.

African craft
The mtepi, of the Lamu Archipelago off the coast of Kenya, was a single-masted, matting-sailed vessel originally used for carrying firewood and mangrove poles to Zanzibar.

In general appearance the mtepi resembled an Arab dhow,

The tainui, used by the Maoris on their transpacific migrations.

The mtepi, a matting-sailed vessel from the coast of Kenya.

with its sharply raking bow and stern and gaily adorned rudder. The hull, however, was built with planks sewn together with coir twine and caulked from inboard by coir fibers hammered into the seams. Then it was covered with bands of coir fiber and palm-leaf stalks.

When the hull was completed, it was reinforced by rib frames which were lashed inside through holes bored in the planking and then plugged by wooden stoppers. Accommodation for the crew was a palm-thatched cabin aft.

The stem- and sternposts of this unusual vessel were built up with blocks of wood, arranged to overlap—thus giving the necessary rake—and then pinned into position by trenails. This method of ship construction was used by countries where suitable wood for shipbuilding was scarce and could well have been inherited from the ancient Egyptians.

Characteristic of this East African craft were the tassels of palm fiber and the three gaily colored flags adorning the beak-like bow, which in some instances also bore a figurehead and *oculi*. The inherent weakness of the mtepi lay in the piecemeal construction of the stem and stern and in the large, unwieldy sail, which made the vessel awkward to handle except in fair winds.

The single-outrigger canoe is essentially a type of coastal craft used for its lightness and ease of handling among islands where surf and sudden squalls are encountered. Under such conditions the double-outrigger canoe is unsuitable, since the double outrigger can constitute a positive danger when the craft is thrown on its beam ends by a sudden squall or surf and the lee outrigger is suddenly submerged.

Under these conditions the drag of the lee outrigger makes steering difficult and could cause enough strain to destroy the craft. Typical of the single outrigger canoe is the sakalavan of Madagascar. The hull of this fishing canoe is a narrow dugout with a thwartship frame which carries the outrigger and the midship platform from which the frail but fast and seaworthy craft is steered by means of a paddle.

The single-outrigger
sakalavan of Madagascar.

A sailing balsa made of reed bundles, from Lake Titicaca, Peru.

South American craft

The largest Peruvian sailing balsas were used until recently for carrying livestock and passengers and for fishing on Lake Titicaca. They were double-ended, with a crew of two, and capable of carrying up to twelve people. The hull was constructed of two spirally bound reed bundles, twenty feet long, tapered and curved to form the bow and stern. Two smaller bundles were then lashed along each side to provide the necessary free-board. The bamboo masts—either single or bipod—were shipped so that they could be lowered forward when not in use. The sail, woven of totoa matting, laced to a bamboo yard and boom and reinforced by four light bamboo battens, was rigged on the after side of the mast. The balsas last for two to three months only, after which the reeds and lashings rot and fall to pieces.

The jangada, a log-built
sailing raft used by
fishermen in Brazil.

The jangada is a primitive but specialized raft used by
Brazilian fishermen. The rectangular dish-shaped hull consists of several lightwood logs, pinned together with long
wooden dowels. The sail is rigged on a free sprit, as on a spritsail barge. On larger jangadas accommodation is a thatched
cabin built on a platform aft, behind which is the crutch into
which the mast is lowered when not in use. To offset the leeway due to its shallow draught, the jangada carries a center keel
housed in a hardwood casing just aft of the mast, and a long,
narrow-bladed rudder-cum-steering oar is also used.

67

WARSHIPS AFTER 1500

The ancient civilizations of Egypt, Greece and Rome recognized that the needs of a fighting ship—speed, room for many men, strength to batter the enemy—differed from those of ships to carry cargo. The distinctions were gradually lost during the dark ages until, by the end of that period, caravels and carracks were used for war, trade and exploration. As the world moved into the new spirit of the Renaissance, even the skills of war were improved and new breeds of fighting ships were born.

During the sixteenth century ships increased greatly in size and armament, the largest being *Henry Grâce à Dieu*—known as *Great Harry*—built by Henry VIII of England in 1514 to meet the growing threat of Spain. This towering, four-

The *Henry Grace a Dieu*, a massive warship armed with 151 cannon.

masted warship of over 1,000 tons was the first vessel known ever to carry top-gallant masts on fore-, main- and mizzenmasts, together with a topmast on the bona-venture. Rebuilt between 1536 and 1539 *Great Harry* was the most advanced war-ship of her time. She had a formidable armament — 21 heavy bronze cannon and 130 medium-sized iron can-non. Her crew were armed with a variety of muskets and grenades. *Great Harry* was more a fortress than a ship, for soldiers were more numerous and important than sailors, at that time.

The galleon or 'Great Ship', probably of Spanish origin and adapted by other countries, was a new type of vessel built to replace the carrack. Her hull was more slender and graceful than that of the carrack with the fore-castle no longer overhanging the bow but built behind a ram-like projection called the beak head. This area housed the crew's toilets — hence the modern sailors' term 'heads'.

Steering was now con-trolled by means of the whip-staff — a vertical extension of the tiller on rollerbear-ings in the 'steersman's hutch', a small cabin sunk in the poop deck. The trees')

Ark-Royal

Armada galleon

69

were erected to protect the sail trimmers and fighting men. Top arming masked the crew from the aim of enemy musketeers and bowmen but provided no other safety. It consisted of two bolts of canvas, three feet six inches wide and painted in red, green, yellow and white, stretched around the waist in the form of a screen. Alternatively, parvesses or scantling were used; these were screens of planks of thin wood painted with shields like the Norse longships.

The sixty-gun *St. Louis* was purchased from the Dutch in 1626 by Cardinal Richelieu, the 'Father of the French Navy'. She was one of the ponderous 'wooden-walls' which superseded the galleon. Cannon were improving and boarding parties became increasingly ineffectual; thus the waist had stout gratings to shield the crew from falling spars and debris, instead of nets to protect them from boarding parties. Rigging was now more complex, sails larger and more functional: they had buntlines and clewlines for furling like the later clippers. The bowsprit now carried a sprit topsail as well as the spritsail;

The Dutch-built *St. Louis*

A 70-gun Dutch fighting ship of the mid-17th century.

fore- and mainmasts carried topgallant sails and the mizzen
—still lateen-rigged—a mizzen topsail.

During the mid-seventeenth century, the Dutch were
developing their own undecorated class of fighting ship: they
had little time for adornment which could be obliterated with a
single broadside. The two gun decks of Dutch warships were
well ventilated by spacious deck gratings, covered with tarpau-
lins in high seas. Dutch ships were generally swifter and
handier than English or French vessels, but of lighter construction. So weatherly and efficient were they that Peter the Great,
ruler of Russia, visited Holland as well as England to study
shipbuilding for himself.

The *Sovereign of the Seas,* launched in 1637, cost the then
enormous sum of £66,000, raised by the Ship Money tax

The *Sovereign of the Seas,* a 1,700-ton warship launched in 1637.

which helped to bring the downfall of Charles I. This ornately carved and gilded, three-masted, three-decked, 1,700-ton warship, with its impressive armament of 102 guns, was said to be 150 years in advance of her time. She was probably the first sailing vessel ever to carry royals above her fore and main topgallant sails and a mizzen topgallant above the mizzen topsail. She also boasted an elaborately carved entry port very similar to that of H.M.S. *Victory,* launched 128 years later. In 1652 *Sovereign of the Seas* was cut down to a two-decker by Peter Pett, son of Phineas, her builder, to increase her weatherliness, and thereafter renamed *Royal Sovereign* to commemorate the restoration of the monarchy.

Contemporary drawings of *Royal Sovereign* by Van de Velde the Elder show carving and gilding probably only equalled by the French, who protected it in battle with matting. The fighting efficiency of warships was beginning to give

1 fore topsail
2 main topsail
3 foresail
4 forecastle (fo'csle)
5 waist (amidships)
6 mainsail (furled)
7 mizzen sail
8 spritsail
  topsail
9 spritsail
10 forestay
11 topmast stay
12 bowsprit
13 spritsail
   topmast
14 shrouds
15 poop
16 taffrail

The *Vasa*,
a 1,400-ton
Swedish warship.

17 gallery
18 cathead
19 ports
20 fairleads
21 figurehead
22 bilge

23 fore topgallant sail (furled)
24 main topgallant sail (furled)

precedence to flamboyancy. In 1703 the Lords of the Admiralty ordered that ship decoration should be cheaper: by
1737 a mere £166.12.0. was allowed on the decoration of a
first-rate ship and only £37 for a sixth-rater. This common
sense legislation had far-reaching effects, for soon the English
man-o'-war became the standard vessel for many maritime
powers.

Representative of this type of warship was the 1,400-ton

The chebek, used by the Algerian corsairs.

Swedish warship *Vasa*, launched before the Royal Palace of Gustavus Adophus in Stockholm on August 10, 1628. Her only adornment was a huge, gilded and snarling lion figure-head, and ferocious-looking gilded lions' heads, set on a blood-red background, at each gunport. Before she had sailed a mile, *Vasa* was struck by a vicious squall, heeled rapidly on her beam-ends and, despite desperate efforts to trim the weight of the cannon, water roared through the open gunports and within minutes *Vasa* plummetted to the bottom. In 1956 she was located, and a complicated salvage operation began. On May 4, 1961, *Vasa* was towed triumphantly to dry-dock at Beckholmen, where her sodden timbers were treated with polyethylene glycol to preserve them. Finally *Vasa* was enclosed in glass and concrete as a unique maritime memorial.

A much later development of the dromon was the chebek, a swift, shallow-draught vessel used by the Algerian corsairs of the seventeenth century. The yacht-like chebeks with their ornately gilded and painted stern and grating deck, carried heavy cannon and were feared for their formidable per-formance in battle and their ferocious crews.

Although efficient sail design was fast rendering oars obso-lete, galleys were used in battle after 1700. Their slow decline was due to their effectiveness against becalmed warships.

The French developed the last type of galley, known as the réale, which carried light cannon in the bow. As with later warships, the captain and officers were housed in luxurious quarters in the stern, while the crew lived between decks as best they could. The anchor-cable locker and ship's store-room were situated forward and served as the hospital in time of battle. A unique feature of the réale was a large room amidships called 'tavern', which served both as a sail locker and a wine shop: wine was as necessary to the crew of these galleys as rum was to the later sailors of thc 'wooden-walls', for their existence aboard was miserable in the extreme. So low were the bulwarks of these fast but unseaworthy vessels that the oarsmen were often rowing up to their waists in water.

The last galley of this type was built in 1720, for by then it was acknowledged that the light hull construction which gave thc galley its speed also made it vulnerable to the cannon of the more stoutly built warships; in 1684, for example, the guns of the French warship *Le Bon* had smashed an entire fleet of thirty-five galleys.

The French réale. The last of these war galleys was built in 1720.

Frigates

In 1793 the fast chebeks of the Bey of Algiers (see pages 74–5) took to attacking American merchant ships in the Mediterranean. In reply, the American Naval Act of 1794 instigated the building of six naval frigates to act as escorts to her merchant ships. One of these, the 2,200-ton *Constitution,* was launched, on October 21, 1797. Her captain during the War of 1812 was William Bainbridge, who, on October 31, 1803, had the misfortune to run the U.S. frigate *Philadelphia* aground off Tripoli, and had been forced to surrender to the gun boats of the piratical Bey.

On December 29, 1812, cruising off Bahia, South America, was the British frigate H.M.S. *Java,* under Captain Henry Lambert. She sighted *Constitution* and hoisted recognition signals; they were not answered and Captain Lambert showed his colors. The welterweight *Java* (forty-nine guns) and the light-heavyweight *Constitution* (fifty-nine guns) then joined battle. A musket-ball smashed into Bainbridge's leg, causing him to reel across the quarterdeck. It saved him from a cannonball which would have killed him outright. He continued to direct the battle propped against the bulwark.

Captain Lambert now tried to thrust *Java* against *Constitution* in a desperate effort to board her, but Bainbridge

The defeat in 1812 of the 49-gun British frigate *Java* (*left*) sunk by the heavier American vessel *Constitution*.

countered this maneuver by blasting *Java* away with furious broadsides. This was the turning point of the engagement. While the badly mauled *Java's* crew — many of them veterans of Trafalgar — were still using short-range, inaccurate, smooth-bore muskets, the Americans were using rifles — probably for the first time in naval warfare.

Java fought on, until her last gun was silenced and she began to sink with her dead and wounded. The British crew and their dying captain were taken aboard *Constitution*, where the sorely wounded Captain Bainbridge ordered his own bed to be brought up on deck for Captain Lambert. As the two captains lay side by side, Bainbridge pressed the hilt of Captain Lambert's sword gently into its owner's numb fingers.

H.M.S. *Java* had been sunk, sixty of her crew killed and 170 wounded. The American losses were only nine men killed and twenty-five wounded. *Constitution*, affectionately known as 'Old Ironsides', remained on active service until 1881 and is now restored and in the Boston Naval Shipyard, where she recalls a mighty past.

Ships-of-the-line

During the latter part of the eighteenth century smooth-bore cannon firing solid shot were reaching the peak of their destructive power. The formidably majestic ship-of-the-line was the most massively timbered sailing warship in history — counterpart of the great capital ships to come.

Not the largest, yet certainly the world's most formidable ship-of-the-line was the 102-gun H.M.S. *Victory,* the flagship of Lord Nelson. Originally built at Chatham Dockyard between 1759 and 1765 and twice rebuilt before the Battle of Trafalgar, *Victory* was made to withstand the shattering power of heavy cannon at close range, her double-layered hull, painted yellow and black, was of stubborn English oak, her 150-foot keel of iron-hard teak; her bottom was copper-sheathed against teredo worm. Such was the bulk of *Victory* that she needed 125 fathoms of nine-inch hempen cable to hold her at a safe depth in deep water.

With the exception of her stern carvings, covered quarter galleries, entry port and figurehead, *Victory* was sparsely ornamented. On the lower gun deck she carried thirty 32-pounders, each of three tons, known from their nine-foot barrels as 'ling nines'. These guns had a range of one and a half miles and each required a crew of fifteen. At 500 yards they could smash an iron ball through three feet of solid timber — the resulting splinter blast being as lethal as a modern fragmentation bomb. The middle gun deck carried twenty-eight 24-pounders, the upper deck thirty 12-pounders, the half deck ten 12-pounders and the forecastle head two 12-pounders and two 68-pound carronades, gaping monsters which fired 300 musket balls at close range and were called 'smashers'. The 102 guns consumed a formidable variety of shot, including grape shot (iron balls in canvas bags), fagot shot (iron cylinders which split into sections), dismantling shot (iron blades on a ring), chain shot (two cannonballs joined by a chain) and langridge (a form of shrapnel used to damage rigging).

Today, *Victory,* now in dry dock at Portsmouth, England, attracts nearly 400,000 visitors a year.

H.M.S. *Victory,* length 226ft., beam 52ft., 2,163 tons; above are the *Ohio* (*left*) and a contemporary French warship.

The U.S. corvette
General Pike.

Corvettes and sloops

The corvette was one class smaller than the frigate; the sloop,
one class smaller than the corvette. Both were light warships
used for reconnaissance work, for convoying and as privateers.
They were the first war vessels to adopt screw propulsion, although they retained their sails and wooden hulls. One of the
first vessels to incorporate the new with the old was the screw
frigate H.M.S. *Arrogant,* designed by J. Fincham of Portsmouth Dockyard, England and launched there in 1848.

U.S.S. *General Pike,* launched in 1813, took only nine
weeks to build. She carried twenty-six 24-pounder cannon and
two short-barrelled 24-pounder carronades. So vastly out of
proportion to the size of her hull was this corvette's spar and sail
plan that it is interesting to compare some of her dimensions
with those of the great clipper ship *Lightning,* (see pages
134–5) which was one of the most heavily sparred and can-
vassed vessels ever built.

General Pike: Length 174ft.; beam 37ft.; mainmast 195ft.
Lightning: Length 244ft.; beam 44ft.; mainmast 164ft.

Both vessels carried skysails on fore-, main- and mizzenmasts.

The sloop has changed in appearance and function, but the first sloops were light warships, smaller than the corvette and frequently used most successfully for chasing smugglers.

The three-masted sloop shown below is a model believed to be that of the 385-ton H.M.S. *Cygnet,* captured from the French in 1779. She carried an armament of eighteen 16-pounder cannon.

Smaller fighting ships

The bomb ketch first appeared in 1682: a broad-beamed vessel converted by removing the foremast to clear space for the heavy mortars. The oaken 'knees' were changed for iron ones, and the deck was strengthened by heavy wooden 'beam bridges' against the shock of the trunnion-mounted mortars which lobbed a high-trajectory, 200-pound spherical bomb (the next most destructive missile known being a 48-pound solid shot). No recoil system of springs or cylinders yet existed: cannon were held by heavy ropes and tackles to prevent them overturning on the gun crews when fired. Even the toughest sailors detested service in a bomb ketch, such was the terrible

A three-masted sloop, probably H.M.S. *Cygnet* (from a model).

A bomb ketch

A gun launch

shock of the short-bar-
relled sea mortars' dis-
charge.

Built by the Swedes for
use against Russia from 1760
to 1790, the shallow gun
launch was the ancestor of
the World War II gun boats.
It was a lug-sail-rigged
vessel which could also be
propelled by oar, and armed
with an 18- or 24-pounder
cannon fired from the plat-
form-like stern, built to
save the crew from running
the gun in and out.

Some ships designed for
fighting were privately
owned, outside of regular
naval forces. The most common of these were the privateers, men-of-war built and
sailed by civilians under
government commissions
which allowed them to prey,
for private gain, on the
vessels of enemy nations.
Many of these fast and smart
vessels slipped beyond a very
thin line to become pirates,
or went into illicit trades
such as slaving and smug-
gling.

During the Napoleonic
Wars many British ships fell
victim to the *chasse-marée*,
a large, decked-in, three-
masted lugger used by French
privateers. These vessels
were fast, armed with up to
ten cannon ranging from

The *chasse-marée*, a three-masted French lugger

swivel guns to 18-pounders, and manned by crews of between forty and seventy-five men.

The American privateer *Prince de Neufchâtel* was an hermaphrodite schooner, that is, she carried both square-rigged and fore-and-aft-rigged sails on both masts. Unlike the lumbering, bluff-bowed wooden warships of her time, this splendid schooner was fast and lean. In March 1814 she snapped up nine British prizes in swift succession in the English Channel. Then, leaving prize crews on board, she put into Cherbourg laden with spoils. She captured six more prizes from June 4 to 10 and later, in the Irish Sea, she captured ten brigs, two sloops, a cutter and a British privateer. Frequently chased by British warships, her speed under an enormous press of sail was often more than twice that of her pursuers.

On December 28, 1814, however, disaster struck. *Prince de Neufchâtel*, sighted in half a gale by three British frigates, started to flee and, indeed, was outstripping her enemies, when suddenly the tremendous stress of her vast sail area sprung her masts. Captured and taken to England, she seemed to prefer death to dishonor, for later she broke her back on the sill of the dock gate as she was leaving for service with the

The American privateer *Prince de Neufchâtel.*

84

The 75ft. *Amistad,* a schooner which carried slaves from Cuba to the United States

British Navy.

The *Amistad,* though smaller than the *Neufchâtel,* was similar in appearance. She was a slaver, engaged in bringing Negroes from Cuba to the United States. In 1839 a consignment of slaves, led by their chief, killed the captain and overpowered the crew, forcing one of them to turn and head the ship for Africa. Short of food, they decided first to put into Long Island to forage. They were promptly captured by a naval detachment. They were acquitted after a two-year trial which much inflamed the slavery question.

In the early seventeenth century the Dutch sailed small, two-masted pleasure craft called jachts in their inland waters. Eventually the ship-wise Dutch decided that the jacht was too small for two masts and built a single-masted vessel from which evolved the cutter, a fore-and-aft-rigged vessel, which origi-

Revenue ship chasing smugglers

nally carried one and sometimes two square-rigged sails. So
fast and handy were the cutters that they became the favored
vessel of Revenue forces and smugglers alike. They also served
as dispatch boats with regular naval squadrons.

The two most notorious English smuggling cutters were
Swift and *Ranger.* The latter was built at Cawsand Village near
Plymouth, England. Armed with twenty-two cannon and
manned by a crew of 100, she was so formidable during the
1780's, that she openly made regular landings of contraband
near Torbay, Devon. The *Swift*, of 100 tons, with sixteen
cannon and manned by some fifty men, also made regular
landings near Torbay, bringing 2,000 casks of spirits and five
tons of tea at a time. In her first year she paid for her building
and running expenses and provided her owners with a
handsome dividend.

These were but two of the many smuggling vessels that
haunted the shores of southern England from 1750 to 1850. To
combat them the hard-pressed Revenue forces had only forty-
four cutters, manned by a total of 1,041 men. The largest of 210
tons and thirty men, was stationed at Colchester, Essex. The
next largest were *Tartar* of Dover, Kent; *Speedwell* of Wey-
mouth, Dorset, and *Rose* of Southampton, Hampshire, each of
190 tons, with twelve cannon and crews of thirty. It is prob-

able that no two of these could have matched *Ranger* or *Swift*.

At this time the English smugglers were extremely powerful; the reason for their immunity lay in the connivance of influential people who enjoyed the huge profits and duty-free luxuries of smuggling.

Two young midshipmen of the Coast Blockade courageously engaged a big band of smugglers carrying kegs along Middle Street, Deal in 1817. The midshipmen fought desperately, but they were eventually forced to take refuge in a nearby shop by a huge mob of townsfolk. Mayor Edward Iggulsden promptly had the midshipmen arrested. At the trial Iggulsden, blatantly ignoring the evidence, jailed them without bail on a capital charge of wounding a number of the smugglers. Luckily for the two young officers, Lord Justice Holroyd intervened and they were released and rewarded with promotions.

The smuggling cutters finally vanished about 1860, discouraged by changing tariffs and a more enlightened public attitude.

One of the most common small naval ships, the brig, was square-rigged on both masts with a fore-and-aft rigged

A cutter, used
by smugglers and
Revenue men alike.

U.S. naval brig of the 18th century.

brigsail on the mainmast (later known as the gaff main-sail). She also carried studding sails ('stuns'ls'), staysails, jib and foresail and, many, like fifteenth- and sixteenth-century ships, a spritsail on the bowsprit to steady the ship's head when running with the wind. Lofty-sparred and sometimes over-canvassed, the brig was a fast and handy vessel, usually armed with fourteen to sixteen cannon and employed both as despatch carrier and privateer.

Probably the last fighting sailing ships were the converted merchantmen which lured enemy subs and raiders during two World Wars. One of these, the 210-ton, three-masted schooner *Mary B. Mitchell,* was built at Carrickfergus, Ireland, in 1892, and looked like a helpless old sea-spinster. While she lay in Falmouth Harbor loading china-clay during World War I the British Admiralty transformed her. Deck-housing which collapsed at the touch of a lever hid 12-pounder guns; she carried a radio transmitter and a gymnasium to keep her hand-picked crew fit for battle. Thereafter she sailed regularly from Falmouth, ostensibly as the dowdy old *Mary Y. José* of Vigo, but in reality a Naval 'Q' or 'Mystery' Ship, designed to destroy German submarines. On December 2, 1916 she sank the German submarine U26 and later, in the Mediterranean, she sank two more in one day, on June 30, 1917.

The *Mary B. Mitchell,* a famous schooner.

After the spurt in technology which saw the caravel and the carrack develop into three- and four-masted vessels with both square and fore-and-aft sails by the end of the fifteenth century, the next period was one of refinement. Ships became longer, larger and relatively narrower, and sails and rigging became more efficient. Many of the improved models, such as the galleon (page 69), were cargo ships as well as warships; in fact it was the rule for cargo vessels to be heavily armed in an age when piracy was common.

The East Indiamen

The Dutch *fluyt,* a round-sterned vessel with rather flat bottom, originated in this period and from it developed the Dutch East Indiamen. Built in 1717, *Geertruyd,* of 100 tons last (cargo-carrying capacity), 130 feet overall and manned by a crew of 180, belonged to the Dutch East India Company. On her third charter she made voyages to Batavia in 1718, 1723, 1727 and 1731.

The 130ft. Dutch East Indiaman *Geertruyd.*

The British East Indiaman *Essex*, with her suit of 63 sails.

Essex was famous as the greatest sail-carrier ever built, with a suit of sixty-three sails. On the mainmast alone she carried twenty-one sails, including three set above the skysail — the 'cloudscraper', 'moonraker' and 'stargazer'. She was probably the first camouflaged vessel, having one side painted differently from the other to confuse pirates.

Formed by Royal Charter in 1600, the British East India Company eventually became the most powerful organization of its kind ever to exist. By 1808 it had fifty-four ships, aggregating 45,342 tons, which sailed from London to India and China. A typical outward-bound cargo included household goods, watches and wines; a return cargo, spices, sugar, opium and ivory. In 1795, incidentally, the Company was able to lend the Admiralty fourteen of its fine ships and 13,000 men.

Their captains were the elite of the maritime world, entitled to a thirteen-gun salute and a guard of honor on the arrival of their ships. They were also the wealthiest sailors of their day, making as much as £10,000 in a round voyage. While their pay

The *Warren Hastings,* a
British East Indiaman
captured in 1805 by the
French frigate
Piémontaise

was only a token £10 per month, they received unheard-of privileges and perquisites—the most profitable of which was that of shipping out fifty tons of their own trade goods and bringing back twenty tons.

While the East Indiaman was anchored off Deal awaiting the homeward-bound tide for London, the Revenue boarding officer would be splendidly wined and dined by the captain, whose contraband in the meantime was being loaded into the smuggling luggers of Deal. Then the luggers often made straight for the nearest enemy privateer to sell the information that a fat prize lay in the offing.

The richest prizes on the ocean, East Indiamen were, however, no easy prey: the biggest, 1,200 to 1,500 tons, carried forty to fifty cannon, a highly competent chief gunner and well-trained gunner's mates. In 1804 three British East Indiamen, leading a fleet of fifteen, fought off a French squadron consisting of a 74-gun ship and three fine frigates.

Equally gallant but less fortunate was the 1,200-ton East Indiaman *Warren Hastings,* with a crew of 196 and forty-four cannon. Homeward bound from China to Portsmouth, she was attacked by the French naval frigate *Piémontaise* on June 21, 1805. *Warren Hastings* was the bigger ship but had only about half the crew of the enemy frigate.

Warren Hastings fought mightily but the outcome was inevitable, for the French naval frigates of that period were the finest in the world—copied for their excellence by all the great maritime powers, including America. After a bitter battle of five hours, *Warren Hastings,* with many of her crew dead and wounded and her foremast shot away, was towed off in triumph by the French. The sailing qualities and power of *Piemontaise* can be assessed from the fact that in only a moderate breeze and carrying only three single-reefed topsails, foresail and mizzen staysail, she towed her 1,200-ton, heavily laden prize at a constant seven-and-a-half knots.

The last of the East Indiamen was probably *Elizabeth,* which left the Thames for China in the spring of 1833 and finished her voyage in Halifax on August 18, 1834—the same year that the East India Company's charter ended, largely due to public disapproval of its monopolistic powers.

Before the clippers came

The logical successors to the Indiamen, from a design viewpoint, were the Blackwall frigates that followed them in the high-class trades to the East and Australia, and the Yankee packets which dominated the rich North Atlantic liner services after 1818. These two types had much in common: both looked square and solid above the water, capable of standing up to a good blow, but often had surprisingly fine lines in the underbody to allow a good turn of speed.

A late example of this type is the massive 2,500-ton *Marco Polo*, built at St. Johns, New Brunswick, in the middle of the nineteenth century. Noted for her massive pitch-pine timbering, she was purchased by James Baines and fitted out as a passenger ship, her accommodation was luxurious: the dining saloon, for instance, had a maple ceiling and pilasters panelled with mirrors and coins from every country of the world.

Most captains thought the *Marco Polo* too ponderous for record breaking. The notorious James Nicol 'Bully' Forbes

The *Marco Polo*, built 'square as a brick': interior length 185ft., beam 38ft., over 2,500 tons.

94

The *Northfleet,* struck and sunk by a steamer off Dungeness in 1873.

saw, however, that the tremendous timbers and mighty masts of *Marco Polo* would allow her to be driven as few ships could be.

Forbes reached Australia from Liverpool in the record time of sixty-eight days, beating the steamer *Australia* by a week. 'Bully' Forbes drove her under full canvas through roaring gales, through the waves instead of over them, making the fantastic run of 1,344 nautical miles in four days. On one occasion frightened passengers crept from flooded cabins to beg 'Bully' Forbes to reduce canvas before he drove the ship clean under. Forbes laughed in their ashen faces and roared: 'We'll go to Hell or Melbourne!' Thereafter he padlocked the main sheets and stood over them with a revolver in each hand.

Built at Northfleet on the Thames in 1853, the speedy 951-ton *Northfleet* saw notable service as a passenger and troop-ship, carrying troops to the Black Sea during the Crimean War and later between London and Hong Kong. In 1858, com-manded by the excellent Benjamin Freeman, *Northfleet* caused a considerable stir in maritime circles by making the passage from Start Point, Devon, to Hong Kong in the remarkably short time of eighty-eight days and seven hours. The same year, 300 miles from Lands End, she rescued nine men from the shattered Southampton brig *Hebe,* homeward bound from Alexandria.

On the ill-omened day of Friday, June 13, 1862 the sea, as if in belated revenge for being baulked of its victims, wrought havoc with *Northfleet.* Outward bound from London to Hong Kong, she ran into squalls and giant seas, which pooped her twice — the most deadly assault any ship can survive.

Then, in January 1873, while waiting in the lee of Dungeness for a storm to subside, she was struck in the bow by a hit-and-run steamer. Despite all efforts, *Northfleet* sank in twenty minutes, carrying 293 emigrants with her. The ship responsible, the Spanish *Murillo,* was later identified by her damaged bow, although her name had been painted over. All British ships were compelled to show their name on the stern and both sides of the bows as a result of this tragedy.

The *Tweed,* a converted steam frigate, length 285ft., beam 39ft., 6ins.

The *Tweed* had a most unusual history. She was originally a steam paddle frigate named *Punjaub,* built for the Indian Marine and powered by two 700-hp engines. She was armed with ten 68-pounders and saw notable service in the Crimean War, the Persian War and the Indian Mutiny.

The Indian Marine was absorbed by the British Royal Navy, and *Punjaub* was subsequently purchased by the shipowner John Willis, who converted her into a full-rigged sailing ship. In 1863, she laid the Persian Gulf telegraph cable. Then refitted in Bombay as a passenger and troopship, she had all the virtues of a prime clipper after conversion and was fast in most conditions, under the driving leadership of her master, Captain Stuart. Finally, dismasted in a gale, she was towed into Port Elizabeth and broken up.

The clipper ship
Ships like the *Tweed* were the immediate ancestors of the true clippers, which developed almost simultaneously—and independently—in Britain and the United States. There is no exact definition of a clipper, but they all shared certain characteristics, most notably, ends which were sharper and with hollower curves than any ships before them, greater

The *Nightingale,*
a three-masted
American clipper.

97

Flying Cloud, 232 ft. long, beam 41 ft.

ratios of length to beam, lofty spars to carry great spreads of canvas, and large crews to handle the sails smartly.

The first American clippers, like the *Rainbow* and the *Sea Witch,* were built in New York for the rich tea trades to China, but in a few years the California gold rush was using all the fast ships that could be built. One of the finest and fastest was the famed *Flying Cloud,* built by Donald McKay at East Boston in 1851. On her maiden voyage she became the first ship ever to round Cape Horn from New York to San Francisco in under 90 days, and three years later she became the only ship ever to do it twice.

By that time the steamers of two oceans, with the Panama Railroad to connect them, were taking the cream of the California trade, but sail was supreme in the newest gold rush, from Europe to Australia. The Yankee shipbuilders, notably Donald McKay, were ready to build fine clippers for the British lines which dominated on the long Australian run. The *James Baines* was a luxuriously appointed vessel of 2,275 tons,

98

built in 1854 by McKay and named for her British owner.

Her long, sharp, rakish bow was adorned with a figurehead of Mr. Baines; her stern has been judged 'perfect' by the most exacting purists. Her masts and ·sparring were immensely heavy, for she carried 13,000 square yards of canvas in a single suit of sails. The crew lived in a spacious fo'c'sle, while abaft the foremast was a roomy deckhouse leading to the luxurious passenger accommodation. She made her most famous passage under Captain MacDonald, leaving Britain on December 9, 1854 and arriving at Melbourne in the splendid time of sixty-three days. She carried 700 passengers, eighty of them first class, and 1,400 tons of cargo and 350 sacks of mail, which under a penalty clause she had to deliver within sixty-five days.

The spectacular end of *James Baines* came on April 22, 1858. While she was discharging cargo at Liverpool, smoke was seen coming from her main hatch. The fire ran through the ship with devastating speed, and by nine o'clock that night the *James Baines* 'resembled a huge floating cinder'.

The 2,275-ton *James Baines,* length 260ft., beam 44ft., 9 ins.

1 foremast	12 fore upper topsail	17 main lower topsail
2 mainmast	13 fore topgallant	18 main upper topsail
3 mizzenmast	14 fore royal	19 main topgallant
4 bowsprit	15 staysail	20 main royal
5 jibboom	16 mainsail	21 main skysail (furled)
6 martingale		22 mizzen crojack
7 flying jib		23 mizzen lower topsail
8 outer jib		24 mizzen upper topsail
9 inner jib		25 mizzen topgallant
10 fore course		26 mizzen royal
11 fore lower topsail		27 studding sails

The famous American clipper *Lightning* was also built as a passenger and emigrant ship in 1853–54 by Donald McKay for James Baines. Built like an axe to cleave the water, *Lightning* was a long, narrow ship with a finely molded bow which blended classically into the sheerline and cutwater. The figurehead was a goddess bearing a golden thunderbolt in her outstretched hand. Even in an era of over-sparred ships, her masts and yards were awesome. Her mainmast was 164 feet from truck to deck, foremast 151 feet and mizzenmast 115 feet. Her massive mainyard was ninety-five feet long, and her lower studdingsail boomed sixty-five feet. Her sail area was enormous: a total of 13,000 square yards of canvas included a moonraker crowning her mainmast, a distinction shared only by the *James Baines*.

The *Lightning*, length 244ft., beam 44ft., 1,468 tons

Red Jacket, a rival clipper to *Lightning,* length 260ft., beam 44ft., 2,460 tons

Designed by the famous Boston ship designer Samuel H. Pook and built by George Thomas of Rockland, Maine, *Red Jacket* was named after the famous Indian chief whose resplendent figurehead she bore. Intended as a rival to *Lightning* and launched just a few days before her, *Red Jacket* was the larger but her lines were less clean.

These two great ships made history in their transatlantic race of 1854. *Lightning* left Constitution Wharf, Boston, on January 10 and *Red Jacket,* commanded by the famous American packet captain Asa Eldridge, left New York the following day; both ships arrived at Liverpool on January 23. During the race these two magnificent 'flyers' both reached speeds of eighteen knots, *Red Jacket* logging twenty-four-hour runs of 413, 374, 371, 343 and 300 nautical miles, while *Lightning* achieved 436, 328, 312 and 306 nautical miles. *Red Jacket* logged the total of 2,020 nautical miles in six days, a feat surpassed only by the *Cutty Sark.*

A composite iron-
and-wood hull

Composite ships

The American clippers were almost entirely of wooden construction, and their era was ended within a few short years, before the Civil War. Britain's greatest feats in the clipper field came later, owing much to the introduction of iron and, later, steel, into shipbuilding.

The composite ship was invented by John Jordan, son of one of the staff of J. H. MacIntyre and Sons, the Liverpool shipbuilders who launched the two first composite vessels ever built. They were the schooner *Excelsior,* built in 1850, and the barque *Marion MacIntyre,* built in 1851. It was a notable advancement in shipbuilding, for the system combined the strength of iron frames with the flexibility of wooden planking—and strength with flexibility is a prime safety factor in ship construction. Its greatest fault was the galvanic action produced by sea water between wood and metal. This was overcome by fitting rubber insulation between the frames and the planks, which were then secured by yellow-metal corrosion-proof screw bolts with countersunk heads. These were stopped with a special composition after they had been secured. The first composite tea clippers appeared in 1863. They were the famous *Taeping* built by Robert Steel and Co.,

Eliza Shaw built by Alexander Stephen, and *Black Prince* and *Yang-tze*, built by Alexander Hall. The smallest composite barque ever built was the speedy and beautiful *Berean*, constructed by Pile of Sunderland and launched in August 1869. Her net tonnage was 526, she was 160 feet long and had a beam of just over 30 feet.

She was unique in that her 43-foot-long quarterdeck was laid with knotless, buttless four-inch-wide planks of New Zealand Kauri pine. Her deckhousing, topgallant bulwarks, fife rails, skylights, fo'c'sle panelling and ship's boats were all of polished teak.

Although small, she was notably sparred; her mainmast from deck to truck was 116 feet, foremast 112 feet and mizzenmast 93 feet. A dainty but not powerful ship, *Berean* could not be driven like the great clippers of her day and sailed her best in moderate weather with the wind two points abaft the beam. Her best day's run was 315 miles, and she once sailed completely around the world in seventy-six days. At a period when accidents to both ships and crews were commonplace, *Berean's* record was so accident-free that Lloyds of London offered to insure her at a specially reduced premium.

On one occasion she raced with the mighty *Thermopylae* to Tasmania. *Thermopylae* overtook *Berean* south of the Cape of Good Hope — storming along in boisterous winds under her mighty cloud of canvas. The great clipper was soon out of

The composite barque *Berean,* length 160ft., beam 30ft., 526 tons.

sight, but the race eventually finished with the little barque only seventeen hours behind.

Berean was commanded by Captain John Wyrill from the time of her launching until she was sold to the Norwegians in 1896. She spent fourteen years carrying ice from Norway to London, until in 1910 she collided with a steamer and ended her days as a hulk off Falmouth.

The 633-ton *Coonatto*, the smallest composite-full-rigged ship ever built, was 160 feet long with a beam of 28 feet. She was constructed by Bilbe of London in 1863 for the famous Orient Line. Her fine lines, together with Captain Begg's hard-driving capabilities, contributed further to her reputation as 'a wet ship'. She was fast; one splendid passage from Britain to Australia took only seventy days—this after broaching-to off St. Paul's Island where huge seas swept both steering-wheel and helmsman overboard. She was finally stranded on the giant chalk boulders at the foot of Beachy Head, in 1872.

Built as a Blackwall passenger ship in 1866, *Sobraon* was the largest-ever composite ship, with teak planking on iron frames. She was 317 feet long, with a beam of 40 feet, and her sails totalled two acres of canvas. She had a registered tonnage of 2,131, and her hold was 27 feet deep. Yet in spite of this mountain of driving power *Sobraon*, unlike *Coonatto*, was a dry ship. In fact, she was so comfortable and luxurious that doctors frequently recommended her for health cruises. It was said that some of the cures achieved aboard this beneficent ship were little short of miraculous.

She was, however, no floating convalescent home: she

The *Coonatto,* length 160ft., beam 28ft.

The 2,131-ton *Sobraon*, length 317ft., beam 40ft.

could reel off a steady sixteen knots hour after hour and was probably the crack vessel of her time. During one voyage she covered 2,000 nautical miles in one week, while her best day's run was 340 nautical miles — both feats which few steamers of her time, or even later, could hope to equal. *Sobraon* was indeed a singular ship, for she carried her own animals for fresh meat, milk and eggs. She also carried several tons of ice and a fresh-water condenser — an almost unheard of luxury in those days. And she was as seaworthy as well-found, for in 1889, while north of the Crozets, she ran into hurricane-force squalls, which ripped her great sails to snapping 'Devil's bull-whips' and huge seas which swept away the entire length of the port bulwarks, together with a ship's boat and davits, and flooded the passenger accommodation.

When the wind dropped after three days, *Sobraon* rolled so violently in the huge swells while the damage was repaired that, if not for the magnificent order of her standing rigging, her masts would have gone clean by the board.

After her last trip in 1891, she became an Australian Government reformatory ship for twenty years. Then she was refitted as a training ship for boy seamen of the Royal Australian Navy.

The famous tea clipper *Cutty Sark,* built in Scotland in 1869, length 212ft., beam 36ft., depth 21ft., 921 tons net weight

The *Cutty Sark,* of composite build and the only clipper of any kind still in existence, was designed by Hercules Linton for John Willis, and certainly owed something of her form to Willis's *Tweed* (page 97). She was built at Dumbarton, Scotland, for the tea trade in 1869, just as that trade, in sail, was doomed by the opening of the Suez Canal. A mere 921 tons net, 212 feet long with a beam of thirty-six feet, *Cutty Sark* carried a skysail on her lofty mainmast, divided topsails on all her masts and upper and lower studdingsails on her foremast and mainmast. Her slender lines and discreet decoration made her a thoroughbred indeed. As a tea clipper she was often beaten by *Thermopylae*—a clipper of such phenomenal sailing power she could 'ghost' at seven knots in airs so light that they would not extinguish a naked candle burning on her deck. However, *Cutty Sark* became supreme in establishing unbeaten records of sixty-seven, sixty-nine and seventy days from Sydney and Newcastle, Australia, to the English Channel in the Australian wool trade. She now lies in dry dock at Greenwich, a memorial to the finest breed of ships the world has seen.

After the clippers, I: the 'down-Easter'

Once the term 'clipper' was part of the language, it became, at least for many laymen, the favored name for any square-rigged ship. But probably no real clippers were built in America after 1860, and very few anywhere much after 1870. The need for fast, lofty-sparred sailing ships was gone by then, and steamers had the cream of the trade between major ports. Sail might survive in grimy trades and to primitive ports where expensive steamers could not afford to wait for cargo, but it had to be cheaply built and cheaply run. Hulls had to be more boxy and capacious, and speed no longer commanded a premium under sail.

American square-riggers after the Civil War were almost all of the type known as 'down-Easters' after their birthplace 'down East' in New England, mostly in Maine. If they had less fancy work than the clippers, and were rigged for smaller crews, they were still fine and handsome ships that performed well in the trades left to them and did it at freight rates that would have bankrupted a clipper.

One of the finest full-rigged ships ever built in America, the *Henry B. Hyde*, launched at Bath, Maine, in November

The 2,463-ton *Henry B. Hyde*,
length 268ft., beam 45ft.

107

1884, was of 2,583 tons, 268 feet long, with a beam of forty-five feet. Under Captain Phineas Pendleton III, a notorious driver of both ships and men, she was known as a 'damned Yankee hot-box'.

A hard, occasionally brutal man, Captain Pendleton was also a splendid seaman, for during her maiden voyage from New York to San Francisco in 1885 *Henry B. Hyde* lost her foremast and main topgallant mast in a heavy squall in the Doldrums. Undeterred, Captain Pendleton re-rigged her at sea and reached San Francisco after 124 days. She loaded wheat there and reached Liverpool ninety-six days later, returning to New York against head winds in the magnificent time of twenty-three days. This remarkable voyage firmly established the reputation of both ship and master among merchants. After eight voyages *Henry B. Hyde* was taken over by Captain Phineas Pendleton Jr., eventually to become a coal carrier.

Leaving New York on February 11, 1904, she was driven ashore during a full gale. After being refloated, she ran aground again, broke in two and became a total wreck.

Another step toward economy was the simplification of rig, represented by the bark and the barkentine, which allowed ships to be handled by still smaller crews. The bark was a vessel of from three to five masts, square-rigged on all but the aftermost one, which was fore-and-aft-rigged. The barkentine, at the other end of the scale, was square-rigged only on the foremast, all others were fore-and-aft-rigged.

The *Gatherer* was a three-masted, 1,509-ton 'down-East' bark built for the Pacific grain trade. Like the ships themselves, whose softwood construction gave them short life expectancy, the crews were often regarded as expendable and worked beyond endurance, being brutally beaten and even killed. The men who were available for this work were not of the highest type, either, and it was perhaps inevitable that the masters and mates were often known for cruelty and sadism.

Gatherer, under the demoniac sway of skipper John Sparks, became the infamous 'Bloody Gatherer', queen of the 'blood boats'. Off Cape Horn, a Scandinavian sailor scrambled aloft to the royal yard, cursed Sparks roundly and jumped to his death. Another sailor cut his throat and a third was shot by the mate, 'Black' Charley Watt.

The *Gatherer*, a three-masted barque, length 208ft., beam 40ft., built for the Pacific grain trade and ruled by a notably cruel captain, John Sparks, and his brutal mate, 'Black' Charley Watt

The ultimate American contribution to commercial ocean sail was the large cargo schooner. The Dutch had used schooner-rigged vessels in the middle of the 17th century, but the real perfection of the rig and of the hull forms that went with it took place in America, to the extent that it is often thought to be of American origin.

An early example is the Marblehead schooner, which may have developed by about 1750 from Chesapeake Bay types. The Marblehead type was a fast, two-masted, fore-and-aft-rigged vessel, from 60 to 80 feet overall and up to 90 tons displacement. In time of war she could be armed with eight to twelve 10-pound cannon and would carry a crew of 30 or 40 hands; normally she was used for fishing or trading, with much smaller crews.

From the time of the Revolution, schooners always outnumbered square-rigged ships in America, and carried most of its trade. Their numbers even grew as square-riggers declined, because of their great economy: a large schooner, in the later days, might by manned on the scale of 'one captain, one cook, and one man to each mast'.

Maine was notable for its fine wooden four-masted schooners, and a typical ex-

109

A Marblehead schooner

ample was the fore-and-aft-rigged *Helen Barnet Gring*. This clipper-bowed flush-decker was designed by J. J. Wardwell, of Rockland and built by R. L. Bean at Camden.

The *Gring* was an offshore trader carrying both deck and hold cargoes, with a gross tonnage of 1,226, and an overall length of 203 feet. She was launched on July 29, 1919 in Japanese style: garlands of red roses were thrown and white pigeons released to mark the occasion. Her cargoes were, less romantically, phosphates and fertilizer (goat manure).

Sailing from Norfolk to Calais, Maine, loaded with coal, the *Gring* rammed the three-masted New London schooner *William Booth*, at 1 a.m. on April 26, 1928, near the Vineyard Shoals, so violently that *William Booth* sank in five minutes. The crew of five were taken aboard the badly damaged *Gring*, which was forced to anchor and summon the Coast Guard for a tow into Boston.

At this period the cargo schooners were fighting a losing

The *Helen Barnet Gring,* a four-masted schooner built in Maine.

battle with steamships as bulk carriers and, after a short spell of carrying coal, the *Gring,* with many other schooners, was laid up at Boothbay, Maine, in 1932. Five years later she was recommissioned and, in 1940, loaded with goat manure, she tore out her bottom on Cayo Verde, Cuba. Her last moments were marked with untimely comedy, for the mate, bored with waiting, took to the rum bottle and turned his revolver on the captain's chickens.

As in almost any field of technology, so with schooners there was the urge to build them bigger, apparently on the assumption that bigger ones would also be better ones. So while three- and four-masters, at or near their practical size limits, continued to be built, as was the *Gring,* even after World War I, the more ventursome builders began in the 1880's to turn out large schooners with five or more masts.

These larger vessels shared most of the characteristics of their smaller sisters: boxy hulls with flat bottoms, rather blunt ends and an upward sweep to the forward sheer which,

111

The five-masted *John B. Prescott.*

while it made them perhaps somewhat drier than they would otherwise have been, also gave them the look of a ski slope. On the ways or lightly laden they looked clumsy, and many of them were, but the best of them had a surprising grace when deeply loaded; the worst were floating monstrosities.

Their success may perhaps be judged by the number of each type to be built, and the dates of the last. There were 56 five-masters built between 1888 and 1920, ten six-masters between 1900 and 1909, and a single seven-master. Only the latter, built in 1902, was a total failure that never inspired—or merited—repetition, but apparently none of them was as successful as the four-masters which continued to come down the ways in Maine for many more years.

The first of the five-masters was *Governor Ames,* of 1,778 tons gross which, following in the wake of her betters, sailed from New York via Cape Horn to San Francisco. The ferocious gales and cliff-like gray-beards of the Horn were successfully faced and ridden.

The two largest of the five-masters were the *Nathaniel T. Palmer,* 2,440 tons gross and the *John B. Prescott,* 2,454 tons gross, both of which were launched in 1898. A few six-masters, cheaply built, wooden 'utility' ships, appeared in 1900: these included the *George W. Wells,* 2,970 tons gross of Boston and the *Eleanor A. Percy,* 3,401 tons gross of Bath, Maine. The largest of the six-masters, and certainly the longest wooden ship to ever carry cargo, *Wyoming,* was built at Bath in 1909 to carry 5,000 tons of coal, manned only by a crew of twelve. This giant, 3,730-ton schooner was lost in March 1924 after leaving Chesapeake Bay with a cargo of coal.

The steel schooner *Thomas W. Lawson* was the only seven-masted schooner ever built, and she emphasized the impracti-

The 3,730-ton *Wyoming,* length 329ft., beam 50ft.

cability of such huge, many-masted crafts. American seamen hated her for she was as ponderous in her movements as an old-time wooden ship-of-the-line, and even harder to handle.

Designed by Mr. B. B. Crowninshield of Boston and built as a coal-carrier by the Fore River Shipbuilding Company of Quincy, Massachusetts, she was launched in 1902. Her composite masts were 195 feet from truck to deck, the topmasts being of wood and the 135-foot lower masts of steel. When fully loaded she drew 23 feet of water. When sailing light, in ballast, she drew only 13 feet and had such great freeboard that it was impossible to tack her across a stiff breeze.

The total sail area of the *Thomas W. Lawson* was approximately 4,445 square yards, just a little over one-third of the sail area of some of the earlier clippers which were a quarter her size. *Thomas W. Lawson*—a disappointment to all—had a short life, for she was lost in the entrance to the English Channel in 1908.

The 5,218-ton schooner *Thomas W. Lawson*, length 404ft., beam 50ft.

The *Werner Vinnen,* a five-masted steel schooner built in Germany.

Prompted largely by economic necessity, Germany followed America in the building of large, multi-masted schooners, and in 1922 a fleet of five-masted steel schooners, equipped with auxiliary power in the form of surplus diesel engines taken from World War I submarines, was built for the firm of Vinnen of Hamburg.

One of this fleet, *Werner Vinnen,* 1,859 tons gross, plied the South American trade route until 1936. She was remarkable for her unique sail-plan of square-rigged sails on her fore- and mizzenmasts — a rig which classified her, more or less, as an hermaphrodite schooner.

After the clippers, III: iron and steel ships
The first iron ships were of 300 to 600 tons, but as the demand for greater cargo-carrying capacity grew, so did their size. Stronger and more durable than wood or composite ships, early iron ships were more accident-prone. When overloaded, as ships frequently were, they rolled tremendously in rough weather and, being stiff, came back with a mighty jerk which

threw a great strain on the ponderous iron masts and yards. Often the wire standing-rigging snapped and the ship was dismasted. Designers working with the unfamiliar new material may have overrated its strength and underrated its stiffness; as with any new method or material, there were lessons to be learned.

Patriarch was considered the finest iron ship of her time, with luxurious accommodation for forty passengers. The masts and rigging, designed by Walter Hood, were revolutionary: topmasts and lower masts were now in one piece, while the topgallant masts could be telescoped into the topmasts— a safe and easy method of reducing topweight in heavy weather. This innovation more than proved its worth, for although *Patriarch* carried heavy spars, including double topgallant yards at fore- and mainmasts and a full suit of studdingsails, she was never dismasted in twenty-nine years of service between England and Australia. Her sea-keeping qualities were superb, and she was fast. On her maiden voyage, from London to Sydney, with forty passengers and 1,400 tons of general cargo aboard, she took only seventy-four days, setting a record for an iron ship. Her best day's run was 377 nau-

The iron ship
Patriarch, length 221ft.,
beam 38ft., depth 22ft.,
1,405 tons.

tical miles, and her best week's run 2,060 nautical miles. She was finally wrecked south of the River Plate in 1911.

Tillie E. Starbuck, America's first iron full-rigged ship, had a deadweight capacity of 3,750 tons. She was 270 feet long with a beam of 42 feet. Her bowsprit and hollow masts were of steel reinforced with angle iron, and her suit of sails included three skysails bent to standing yards, a double topsail and a single topgallant sail.

Tillie E. Starbuck was something of a disappointment, being much slower than many of her wood-built contemporaries. She finally foundered off Cape Horn in 1907.

Mermerus, with a registered tonnage of 1,671, was a most beautiful and successful clipper. She could carry 10,000 bales of wool worth £130,000, and delivered her cargoes as regularly as clockwork. She once reached Melbourne in sixty-six days. Ships tend to deteriorate with age, but not so *Mermerus,* for she maintained her fine performance to the end of her life—even after being sold to Russia in 1897. In 1904 she made a passage from Cardiff to Adelaide in seventy-three

The *Tillie E. Starbuck*

117

days, and in the following year sailed from Adelaide to the Needles, Isle of Wight, in sixty-nine days.

Her end came on Novermber 29, 1909 when, after leaving Frederickstadt with a cargo of timber for Melbourne, she ran aground in dense fog near Christiansand. After being refloated she was found to be too badly damaged for repair and was sold to the shipbreakers in April 1910.

At 2,000 tons it was said that the *Wavertree* was too big for a three-masted ship. Completed in December 1885, she was first named the *Toxteth* and not until July 1888 was she renamed the *Wavertree*. At first she worked as a cargo carrier, traveling around the Cape of Good Hope to India or Australia and bringing home jute and grain. By 1892 she had been to New York, Rio, Mauritius and Chile.

Mermerus, a 1,671-ton wool clipper.

Wavertree, length 279ft., beam 40 ft.

This meant going around the Cape the hard way—from East to West—against the winds. Her sailing days ended in 1910. In August, 200 miles south of Cape Horn, she was caught in a gale and most of her sails were ripped away. She was refitted at Montevideo and set sail again only to have her mainmast and fore and mizzen topmasts destroyed that December.

The era of the sailing ship was over, and it was felt that the *Wavertree* was not worth the expense of repair. In April 1911 she was towed to Punta Arenas where she spent 37 years as a storage hulk. From 1948 to 1968 she was used as a sand dredge, and in November 1968 she was acquired by the South Street Seaport Museum in New York, where she remains today.

Few vessels had such a varied and unusual career as the six-masted American barquentine *E. R. Sterling.* Originally built as the iron, four-masted *Lord Wolseley* by Harland and Wolff of Belfast in 1883, she was 308 feet overall, with a beam of forty-three feet. Dismasted off Cape Flattery in 1903, she was written off by the underwriters and acquired by C. E. Peabody of Vancouver who had her re-rigged as a six-masted barquentine—square-rigged on the foremast but otherwise fore-and-aft-rigged. This made her slower, but easier to handle, and

The 2,578 ton *E.R. Sterling*

allowed her crew to be reduced from twenty-eight to seventeen.

In 1910 the barquentine was purchased by a well-known American clipper-ship master, E. R. Sterling, who converted her into a modern floating home complete with motor launch and car. On July 4, 1927, she lost her main- and mizzenmasts in a gale off the Falkland Islands. On September 4, 1927 she was again dismasted, near the Cape Verde Islands and the first mate was crushed to death.

E. R. Sterling eventually limped into the Thames after a passage of 286 days out from Adelaide. Almost a floating wreck, she was sold for £4,000 to the Sunderland shipbreakers.

Discovery of the Bessemer and open hearth processes in the mid-19th century introduced steel as an economical material for large structures, both stronger and lighter than the iron which by then was common in European shipbuilding (America had plenty of timber for wooden ships, but Europe's forests had been denuded by centuries of naval warfare, so timber there was scarce and costly and new materials were more readily accepted). By the 1880's most new ships in Europe were of steel; only the most conservative owners and builders turned out new iron ships then.

Built for the Californian grain trade in 1886, *Balclutha* (Gaelic *bal* = town; *clutha* = Clyde) had a gross tonnage of 1,689, and a cargo capacity of 2,660 tons. She was driven by a suit of twenty-five sails and manned by a crew of about twenty-six hands. For thirteen years she carried cargo all over the world. In 1899 she was sold to a San Francisco lumber company. She then served in the Alaskan salmon trade and, after being wrecked in 1904, she was sold to the Alaskan Packers' Association and renamed *Star of Alaska*. Finally she was restored in 1954 and is today preserved by the San Francisco Maritime Museum Association.

The *Balclutha*,
length 301ft., beam 38ft.
6ins., 1,689 tons.

By the time steel became more economical than timber in America, the day of the sailing ship was done, so very few large steel sailers were built here.

Dirigo, known also as 'The Mighty Dirigo', was America's first all-steel sailing vessel—a four-masted barque of 2,845 tons register. Designed by J. F. Waddington of Liverpool, England and built by A. Sewall of Bath, Maine, *Dirigo* had a cargo capacity of 4,500 tons, was steered by Waddington screw steering-gear from a steel helmsman's 'caboose' aft and carried the fantastic spread of 13,000 square yards of canvas, which included skysails and single topgallants. Yet in spite of her driving power the great barque's speed was unimpressive. Her greatest fault was that she was almost unmanageable when sailing in ballast. Once, between Hong Kong and Honolulu she positively refused to go about when tacking, forcing her crew on eighty-one occasions to the laborious expedient of wearing ship (i.e., changing from one tack to the other with the ship's stern to wind).

Leaving Seattle with a cargo of barley in October 1915, she was stopped by a British patrol boat off the coast of Scotland on

Dirigo, a 2,845-ton, four-masted barque, length 312ft., beam 45ft.

The *Preussen*,
length 438ft., beam 54ft.
5,081 tons

suspicion of carrying contraband of war. Escorted into Lerwick, *Dirigo* was found to have a German crew member but was permitted to sail after her cargo was confiscated and the German interned. Jack London sailed on her from Baltimore in March 1912 to collect material for his book *The Mutiny of the Elsinore*. On May 31, 1917 she was sunk in the English Channel, torpedoed by a U-boat near the famous Eddystone Lighthouse.

Until about 1850 Germany's merchant fleet was small. But she began to build vessels on British and American lines, until she had some of the finest steel ships ever to exist.

Notable among these ships were those of the 'P' Line, ('P' was their initial letter), which carried nitrates from Chile to

The *France,* a huge five-masted steel barque—the largest sailing vessel ever built —length 418ft., 5,633 tons.

Hamburg. Unique as the world's only five-masted full-rigged ship, was *Preussen.*

Built in 1902, with a registered tonnage of 5,081 and a cargo capacity of 8,000 tons, she was Gothic in her grandeur, with steel masts three feet in diameter at their butts.

Before World War I France attempted to bolster her merchant fleet by building big sailing ships, frequently running them at a loss. One was the five-masted steel barque *France*— the largest sailing vessel ever built.

In 1919 she was chartered to take coal from the Tyne to America, leaving in December in the tow of a number of tugs, the largest of these being the French tug *Joffre.* All the tugs but *Joffre* left *France* almost as soon as she was at sea, and a few days later barque and escort ran into a roaring gale which parted the towing warp. *France* vanished for several days, and it was generally feared that she had foundered. Eventually, however, the battered vessel limped into the Firth of Forth and after repairs, continued across the Atlantic. Finally she was lost at sea after leaving New Caledonia bound for Europe with a cargo of iron ore.

OTHER WORKING SAIL

Fishermen

One of man's earliest involvements with the sea and ships is in the catching of fish for food, and many fine sailing ships have been built for fishing, developing, like all ships, according to their function and environment. At one time, for example, Norwegian fishermen, restricted to fishing in one area, used a small, thirty-foot fembøring, which carried only one sail. Then, in 1857, the Lofoten fishery regulations were amended, and fembørings were enlarged to between forty-four and fifty feet in length, the single mast having a square-rigged mainsail and a square topsail. The sails were either of canvas or homespun russet, and the vessel itself was built of pine or spruce.

The Skerries or Greencastle yawl was not yawl-rigged; the

One of the larger type of fembøring, a single-masted Norwegian fishing vessel, length 44 to 50ft., beam 9½ to 12ft.

A Skerries yawl

A Shetland sixern

name comes from the Scandinavian 'jol', which applied to all double-ended boats. This unusual craft had a uniquely flexible rig, having a hole in each of the three forward thwarts, which permitted its two masts to be stepped in different positions. One method was to step one mast in the bow thwart and the second in the third thwart and then set the sprit foresail, gaff mainsail and a small jib, which made the Skerries yawl the only schooner-rigged fishing craft in the British Isles.

Do-it-yourself boat-building kits are no recent innovation, for the Shetland sixern—so called because it could be rowed with six oars ('slates') when necessary—was shipped from Norway to the Shetlands in kits ready for assembly over a century ago, as suitable timber is scarce in the Shetlands.

The sixern had Norse lines, and was up to thirty-six feet long. The large dipping lugsail entailed dipping the yard around the mast each time the boat changed tack. The helms-

(*Right*) the zulu, a fishing
vessel developed in 1878.
(*Below*) the large, double-ended
Manx nickie.

man controlled the mainsheet
and sat with his boot on the
garboard strake, the plank
next to the keel. When the sixern was driving dangerously
fast, the strake vibrated
strongly under his foot. The
sail would be lowered in-
stantly and hoisted only
when the vibrations ceased.

The zulu combined the
best points of two earlier
Scottish fishermen: the skaf-
fie, which was dry and handy;
and the fifie, which behaved
better in a following sea. She
carried high-peaked lugsails
on mainmast and mizzen, and
a long bumpkin, or spar, to
take the mizzen sheets as in a
yawl. The mainmast could be
lowered aft along the deck to
provide space for the hauling
of herring drift-nets. The zulu
was the fastest fishing vessel
in the British Isles.

The Manx nickie was a
carvel-built fishing craft,
with hardly any sheer, draw-
ing more water aft than forward and unusual in that it
carried a mizzen staysail.
Like Cornish luggers, the
nickie had a sharp stern in
preference to a square tran-
som stern, for ease of
maneuver.

A North Sea
ketch-rigged
sailing trawler

From 1700 to 1900 the ketch was a common sight in European waters—especially the tan-sailed trawlers. Until about 1860 the main fishing ports of Britain were Brixham, Devon, and Barking, Essex. Pollution of the Thames led to the expansion of Great Yarmouth, Hull, and Grimsby, the home of the large trawlers of up to ninety tons. The smaller ones ranged from forty-five to eighty tons, the crews varying from four to eight men. The ketch-rigged sailing trawler was then the finest fore-and-aft-rigged vessel in Europe, its straight-stemmed, gracefully sheered and massively timbered hull being admirably designed to withstand heavy seas and the weight of the beam trawl as it dragged across the sea bed. The crew lived in a cabin aft while forward was the boiler room for the steam capstan which hove up the trawl, two hatch-covered fish holds, an ice store, and the sail locker/storeroom in the bow. The powerful mizzenmast and mainmast raked slightly forward, the latter carrying a gaff-rigged mainsail, maintopsail, jib and foresail, while the mizzenmast—stepped well forward of the rudder head—carried a gaff-rigged mizzen and a mizzen topsail. When becalmed, trawlermen spread a spare sail beneath the trawler's keel to catch the tide and thus keep the trawl moving.

In the first half of the nineteenth century, the North Sea was the world's richest fishing ground, and huge fleets of trawlers often remained fishing continuously on the Dogger Bank for three months at a time and more—a practice known as 'bulk fleeting'. Fast fish cutters raced the catches to the nearest port.

From 1860 to 1910, a fleet of fourteen yawl-rigged well smacks sailed from Aldeburgh, Suffolk, to the Iceland Banks, returning with up to two thousand live cod in their special 'wells'. Yacht-like in their graceful rig, they were the last of a proud tradition, for among their crews were direct descendants of the 'Fisherman Venturers' who, Aldeburgh's Elizabethan chronicles tell us, would 'yearly man fourteen ships to Iceland and the North to bring back thirty to forty thousand cod and ling to the great comfort and relief of the Queen's ministers and subjects'.

Gypsy, a yawl-rigged well smack

Some of the finest sailing fishermen anywhere came out of New England and Nova Scotian ports to fish the Grand Banks of Newfoundland. The ships were always fast, and designers strove to make them faster. During one period in the 19th century, new theories were carried to such extremes that stability and seaworthiness were sacrificed for speed in shallow, over-canvassed boats that were hard to keep upright in sudden squalls. Many of these early clipper schooners were lost with all hands.

Deeply concerned by these events, D. J. Lawlor and others developed the 'plumb-stem' schooner, the most notable of their vessels being *Grampus,* launched in 1886. They were straight-stemmed, with a narrow, elliptical stern, narrower in beam but eighteen inches deeper in hull than the clipper schooners. This gave them a greater grip on the water and thus greater stability.

The plumb-stem schooners later gave way to boats with curved stems, which had first appeared on yachts in the 1890's. Some of these, for greater safety, had no bowsprits and brought the head rigging down to a lengthened foredeck. The first of these 'knockabouts' was built at Essex, Massachusetts in 1902

A 'plumb-stem' schooner of the late 19th century

130

and named *Helen B. Thomas.* She was designed by Thomas F.
McManus.

Many of the later Gloucester schooners were designed by
yacht designers and could outsail yachts of similar size. One
of these was the magnificent *Columbia* of 1923, designed by
W. Starling Burgess. Raced under Captain Ben Pine, she beat
everything else out of Gloucester, lost twice by narrow margins
to the great Canadian *Bluenose* and was awarded the International Fisherman's Cup (which Captain Pine declined) when
the Canadians, losing one race on a protest, refused to complete
the series. On August 24, 1927, she was lost with all hands—
22 men—the greatest single loss among the Gloucester
fishermen.

131

A Dutch whaleship

Whaleships

In 1650, when the British and Dutch were bitterly contesting the whaling grounds off Spitzbergen, the Americans first started whaling from Easthampton, Long Island.

Nantucket later surpassed Easthampton as a whaling port, to be surpassed in turn by New Bedford, which became the greatest and most colorful whaling port of all time—its ships leaving on voyages of up to seven years. For the lucky ones the rewards were great, for they brought back oil and whalebone from right and sperm whales valued at $100,000 and more. In 1862 the New Bedford whaleship *Corinthian* brought back a cargo worth $275,000. Others were less lucky, however, like the *Emmeline* of New Bedford, which after a voyage of twenty-six months returned with a beggarly ten barrels of oil.

These whaleships were square-rigged vessels, of 200 to 300 tons, flush-decked, broad in the beam and with deep holds to stow up to 2,400 barrels of oil. Their masts lacked the graceful rake of the clipper ships, and they could always be recognized from afar by the stains on sails and yards from the brick try-works, where the blubber was boiled down for oil.

The whaleboats used for hunting the whale—unlike the lumpy parent vessel—were lithe and graceful boats of cedar planking, so light that two men could lift one and five oarsmen propel it at up to ten knots. The spare boats were kept on

The *Charles W. Morgan,*
an American whaleship
from New Bedford.

chocks between the main- and mizzenmasts, while five others were slung from davits.

Their main equipment included a mast and spritsail, oars and paddles, harpoons so keen they could be used for shaving, lances for killing the whale, sharp whale-spades for cutting blubber, casks of bread and water, and two large tubs holding 300 fathoms of line for the harpoons.

Many of the whaleships' crews were raw countrymen who had never even seen the sea, and they often found their first encounter with the mighty sperm whale quite overwhelming.

When hunted, the sperm whale is not only ferocious but vindictive enough to smash the whaleboats, snap up their crews and even attack and sink the parent ship. This happened to the Nantucket whaleship *Essex*, rammed and sunk in the Pacific by a sperm whale on November 20, 1820 — an incident on which Herman Melville based his classic *Moby Dick*.

The *Eclipse*, an Aberdeen whaler with auxiliary steam power.

Mail packets

Before the middle of the eighteenth century, the only way to reach the Channel Islands or the Continent from England was by chartering a private vessel or by waiting for a merchantman. In 1781, however, the Government organized a fortnightly mail and passenger service between Southampton and the Channel Islands using smart cutters. One of these was the sleek *King George* which plied between Dover and Calais from 1813–23, when sail gave way to steam. A similar service to America, using small brigs, gave way to the Yankee Black Ball packets at about the same time.

Pilot boats

Cutters were also popular with pilots in Britain, as they were smart-sailing craft which could reach the deepsea vessels quickly. The Bristol Channel pilot cutter *Dyarchy* was one of these, built at Bristol in 1901. Other noteworthy pilot cutters served the North Sea ports.

(*Above*) the Government Channel cutter *King George*. (*Below*) the Bristol pilot cutter *Dyarchy*

135

In America, the pilot boats out of ports like New York, Boston and Norfolk were usually schooners; some of the finest ever to sail. In the early days they might be topsail schooners like the Sandy Hook pilot boat *Anna Maria* of 1820, but later the fore-and-aft-rig was more common. Their sea-keeping abilities were legend, and if 11 of the New York boats were lost in the blizzard of 1888, it is worth noting that 6 others rode out that famous gale at sea.

The Sandy Hook pilot schooner
Anna Maria, length 58ft. 11ins.,
beam 17ft. 3ins., built 1819–20.

Coastal and inland traders

Many special craft were developed to trade along certain coasts, rivers and lakes. Their designs usually reflected local conditions of wind, tide, water depths and other matters—even low bridges—that influenced their operation.

Their special design features did not prevent some of these local types from making long voyages, however, as when the Hudson River sloop *Experiment* became, in 1785, the first United States vessel to reach China. Conversely, not all coasters were of local designs; many were just smaller versions of ships which were built for world-wide trades, and many of these coasters ventured far from home.

The brig (a two-masted, square-rigged vessel) was common in coastal trades. One of its specialized versions was the English collier brig, which first appeared in the seventeenth century, when all coal was sea-borne from Newcastle and Sunderland to London. Large fleets of them plied the North Sea; in the month of September 1675 alone, a thousand collier brigs passed Thameswards through the Yarmouth Roads. A model of the 214-ton *Brotherly Love* is in the Science Museum

The collier brig
Brotherly Love,
length 87ft., beam
24ft.

The snow, a brig-type coastal trader

in London. Built in 1704, she was still working in 1876. Seamen thought collier brigs were the lowest craft afloat. The crew lived in the worst imaginable conditions on the poorest food, luckily for not more than four days at a time.

The *Endeavour,* in which Captain James Cook cruised the Australian coast in 1770, was originally a North Sea collier.

The snow was almost identical to the brig, but instead of a brigsail on the mainmast, she carried a snowsail on the snowmast or trymast. This was an auxiliary spar stepped just abaft the mainmast and secured by an iron clamp to the afterside of the maintop. This prevented the squaresail on the mainmast from being fouled by the hoops of the snowsail as it was hoisted and lowered.

The brigantine often replaced the brig in coastal trades in the later years because, with its schooner-rigged mainmast, it was cheaper to run. One brigantine that made long voyages became the most celebrated mystery ship of all time. She was the American *Mary Celeste,* built in Nova Scotia in 1861 as the *Amazon.* She seemed cursed from the start. Her first three Captains died, went bankrupt and ran her on the rocks. Her owners, fully convinced that she was jinxed, sold her for a fraction of her value. Her next captain promptly ran her aground.

Again she was sold and her new owner, Captain J. H. Winchester of New York, rebuilt, refitted and renamed her. The name he chose was 'Mary Sellars', which a French painter wrote as *Mary Celeste.* On November 7, 1872, loaded with 1,700 gallons of alcohol, she left New York for Genoa. Aboard were the captain's wife, baby daughter and crew of seven. On December 5, the *Dei Gratia* found her sailing erratically between the Azores and Portugal. When boarded, her holds were found dry, her cargo unbroached, her occupants gone. The brig's boat, captain's chronometer and papers were also missing. A box of jewelry and a £5 note remained, and an unfinished letter from the mate to his wife. The last entry in the log was at 8 a.m. on November 25.

There were no signs of violence aboard, but she had evidently been abandoned in a hurry. Her crew were never seen again. She was finally wrecked off Cuba in 1885.

The deserted American brigantine *Mary Celeste.*

The Humber keel, a heavy, single-masted barge.

A Norfolk wherry, length 50 to 60ft., beam 10 to 12ft., draught 2 to 3ft.

The Humber keel carried general cargo on the Yorkshire Ouse and Humber; it was a single-masted barge with a huge squaresail, and a square topsail for use in fair winds. Bluff in bow and stern and equipped with heavy leeboards, the cumbersome keel was worked by two men. Surprisingly, it was a remote descendant of the Norse longship, like a war horse which the changing centuries had bred into a cart horse.

The Norfolk wherry—or keel—was a general cargo carrier on the shallow and labyrinthine waterways of Norfolk. The first was recorded in 1706. A giant, 100-foot wherry with a cargo capacity of eighty-one tons was built around 1890. The hold itself occupied all but a twentieth of the barge's length and was covered with removable two-foot sections of hatch. The remaining space was the wherryman's cabin, which held only a small coal stove, two bunks and two small wooden lockers. Cargo capacity was 20 to 25 tons and included stone, coal, crops, timber and cattle cake.

The forty-foot mast—stepped well forward in a tabernacle—was counterbalanced with one-and-a-half tons of lead to permit lowering at bridges. The huge, tanned canvas mainsail was loose-footed but laced to a heavy gaff.

Despite its cumbersome appearance, the wherry could sail surprisingly close to the wind. When a 'dead muzzler' or head wind prevailed, the wherry had to be poled along by means of a heavy quant, a massive pole, eighteen to twenty feet long, with a steel fork at one end and a 'bot' or shoulder-rest at the other. The Norfolk wherrymen needed their famous strength, for 'quanting' meant setting one's shoulder to the 'bot' and walking the length of the wherry, pushing against wind and tide for mile upon mile.

A famous bygone wherryman was George Applegate of Potter Heigham, Norfolk. He could leave Potter Heigham with a fully loaded wherry at ten o'clock and arrive at Great Yarmouth the same evening, a distance of twenty miles—very often in the teeth of a gale. In their heyday as many as sixteen wherries at a time could be seen loading and discharging at Potter Heigham. In 1950 there were only six wherries in Norfolk, all but one being power-driven.

The true round-bowed Thames sailing barge did not develop until the 1830's. Until then barges were tub-like craft called 'swim headers' (i.e., built with an overhanging bow like a present-day Thames lighter). They became the most highly specialized and efficient cargo carriers ever evolved. Only the wind and two men were required to move a vessel carrying up to 120 tons of cargo. Shaped like a wooden pencil box but chined (squared) at the bilges, they had a draught of six to seven feet when loaded; unloaded they drew a mere two feet and were said to be 'able to sail over a heavy dew'. Their flat bottoms and massive strength enabled them to load and discharge on tidal flats, squat happily on shoals and sandbanks, and even be driven on to a lee shore in an emergency.

The most familiar barge rig was the spritsail used by the 'spritties'. It was an enormous tanned canvas mainsail, stretched diagonally by a heavy spar or sprit; its weight was taken by a strong sling called a 'stanliff', while the peak was supported by a heavy rope at the head of the mainsail, and the

The shallow-draught, spritsail-
rigged Thames sailing barge,
length 80ft., beam 18ft.

142

The 'boomie', a ketch-rigged
Channel barge

entire spar steadied by rope guys known as 'vangs'. The
topmast carried a large topsail laced to a short yard called
the 'tops'l stick'. The mainmast also supported a large foresail
and, for use in light airs, a topmast staysail. The mizzenmast,
stepped well aft, carried a sail with both sprit and boom,
the sheet of the latter being rove through a block on the rudder.
This simple but highly effective arrangement made the
barge extremely nimble in going about, for helm and mizzen
moved simultaneously.

Instead of lowering and reefing the sails in a squall, the
crew merely lowered them partially — known as 'rucking'.

The river barges actually operated throughout the Thames
and its estuary, around the east and south coasts of England,
and across the Channel to Holland and Northern France. A

larger variant, known as the 'boomie' because its ketch main and mizzen sails were rigged with booms and gaffs instead of sprits, was built especially for these short-sea services. The 'boomies' had a capacity of up to 300 tons and also carried an additional jib. A 'stumpie' was a smaller barge with no topsail. All barges, like the Humber keels, carried leeboards to reduce their tendency to drift downwind.

The sailing barges are virtually extinct as cargo boats, but a number have been preserved as yachts and as late as the summer of 1969, ten barges could be found racing in the Medway.

A seagoing development of the Humber keel was the 'billyboy'. Like the keel, it was flat-bottomed, straight sided, round in bow and stern, and always fitted with leeboards. But it also had a deeper sheer and higher bulwarks to fit it for sea service, and was generally larger. It may originally have carried the square rig of the keel, but this gave way to fore-and-aft rig, first as cutter or sloop, and later with the ketch

A ketch-rigged billyboy; this coastal cargo vessel was originally developed from the Humber keel.

rig much like that of the 'boomie' barge. The billyboy was often a family ship, operated by a skipper-owner and crewed by his wife and family.

The Great Lakes cover 95,000 square miles, the world's largest expanse of fresh water, which in some aspects resembles the North Sea and Thames Approaches. Both have narrow, winding channels, dangerous shallows, variable winds, sudden and violent squalls and swiftly rising, steep and ugly seas, short of fetch but lethal of impact. Sailing vessels thus had to be especially designed to meet these conditions. *Griffin*, first of the Great Lakes vessels (1679), was a 60-ton craft modeled on a Dutch North Sea galliot.

As American and Canadian industry and agriculture expanded, bulk cargo carriers became necessary and so it was that Great Lakes schooners like the *E. W. Morrison* were developed. They were graceful and durable two- and three-masters, fore-and-aft-rigged and ranging between 100 and 777 tons. All of them had the special 'Great Lakes rig' to enable them to wear and tack quickly in rapidly shifting winds. Unlike the large coastal trading schooners, these lake schooners had their masts of uneven height, with the mainmast slightly taller and the mizzen much shorter than the foremast.

Salvage and life-saving boats

The nineteenth-century luggers and galleys of Kent and Sussex and the great beach yawls of the east coast all took their

A two-masted English lugger from Deal, Kent.

A Deal galley, length 30ft., beam 5ft.

lines from much older Norse ships. The most famous luggers were from Deal, Kent — notorious as a smuggling town. When smuggling no longer paid, their owners turned to 'hovelling' — anything from salvaging a wreck to looking for ships to pilot in the Channel. Later luggers were up to forty feet overall, two-masted, lugsail-rigged, and carried seven or eight men, who lived in a cramped cabin forward. In February 1866, the Deal lugger *England's Glory* launched off into the teeth of a 'sou'-westerly buster' to the Goodwins and salvaged the tea cargo of the *Iron Crown*. It was a feat of supreme seamanship and daring which earned the crew £7,000 in salvage money. The last lugger was sold in 1925 for a mere £2.10.0.

The Deal galleys were often used for lifesaving. Driven by a huge lugsail, they also had rowing thwarts and were steered by oar as well as by rudder when under sail. Owing to their narrow beam, shallow draught and huge sail, they required nearly half a ton of ballast which had to be quickly shifted to the weather side at each change of tack. Two of these magnificent boats still exist at Deal; they are perhaps the most spectacular and interesting of the remaining sailing craft of Britain.

The East Coast yawl (Norse *yol* = a double-ended, clinker-built boat) was very like the Gokstad Ship. The two-masted, lugsail-rigged yawls were usually up to sixty feet long and manned by some thirty men; they were very fast and saved thousands of lives. The biggest of these was the mighty *Reindeer* of Great Yarmouuth, sixty-nine feet long and capable of sixteen knots. On April 3, 1814 the famous yawl *Jubilee* of Southwold, Suffolk raced another yawl to a salvage job, cutting her rival clean in two, probably on purpose, for her crew were a 'bold, artful, surly, savage race.' Only a few weeks before, the same crew had retaken an English brig from the French and captured a French war lugger.

An East Coast yawl, built on similar lines to the Gokstad Ship and used for rescue work.

Britain's Royal National Lifeboat Institution was founded in 1824 by Sir William Hillary and since that time its lifeboats have saved more lives from the sea than any other organization in existence. Before the advent of the magnificent modern power-driven, radio-equipped lifeboats, the work of RNLI was done by means of 'pulling-sailing' lifeboats, equipped with both oars and sails. These boats, though primitive by modern standards, were still highly specialized craft: they had to be small enough to handle but strong enough to endure the elements at their worst; to be able to free themselves continuously of a crippling weight of water, and be so buoyant as to remain afloat when swamped to the gunwales.

Although they were the most seaworthy and durable boats of their time the sailing lifeboats were much more vulnerable that the modern lifeboats, depending as they did entirely on sail and the strength of their volunteer crews.

One celebrated rescue operation concerned the *Indian*

The Padstow
Lifeboat

1 foremast
2 forelugsail
3 mizzen mast
4 mizzen lugsail
5 gaff
6 truck
7 shrouds
8 reef points
9 staysail
10 halyard
11 sheet
12 helm, tiller
13 rudder
14 stern
15 keel
16 stem
17 bilge keel
18 fender
19 bulwarks

Chief, wrecked on the dreaded Longsand in the Thames
Estuary on January 5, 1881. Bound for Yokohama and commanded by Captain Fraser, she ran aground in a bitter easterly
gale, with blinding snow squalls and vicious surf, which burst
the hull. The crew lashed themselves to the tottering masts
where many soon died of exposure. The captain was crushed
by a falling spar and instantly killed. So great was the horror
of this disaster that the second mate and nephew to the captain,
Howard Primrose Fraser, lost his reason and died after being
taken aboard the lifeboat. Four sailing lifeboats were launched,
one each from Aldeburgh, Clacton, Harwich and Ramsgate.
The brutal seas and wind defeated all the lifeboats except the
Bradford of Ramsgate, under Coxswain Charles Fish, which
was towed to the wreck by the paddle tug *Aid.* One of those
rescued said later that he had felt safer on the wreck, as the
lifeboat had seemed likely to be overwhelmed by every wave.

149

The *Esmeralda,* length 285ft., beam 42ft.

Training ships

In an age of powered vessels it may seem odd that many countries should employ sailing ships to train their seamen. However, since a sailing ship is much more vulnerable to the elements than a powered vessel she demands a great deal more from her crew, including a far greater sense of responsibility, urgency and awareness of danger. Clawing aloft on dizzily reeling masts to fist-in vast areas of wet, wind-swollen, thrashing canvas instills all this—and more.

Belonging to the Chilean Navy and launched in 1954, *Esmeralda* is a four-masted schooner 285 feet in length, with a beam of forty-two feet. Powered by a main auxiliary diesel engine of 1,500 hp, she carries over 3,000 square yards of sail. This magnificent schooner was active from the day she was launched, and between 1954 and 1967 she visited twenty-seven countries. In July 1956 she also took part in the International Training Ship Race from Torbay, Devon to Lisbon.

The winner of the big class of sailing ships was an old British ketch *Moyana,* built as a private yacht (before taxation swept them from the seas) and manned by a crew of sixteen-year-olds. *Christian Radich*, a full-rigged Norwegian ship, was second and *Ruyam* of Turkey third. The *Ruyam* was a fine steel yacht originally built as the J Class racing cutter *Thistle* and re-rigged and re-fitted as a yawl in Germany. In the small-ship class the tiny, six-ton Italian yawl *Artica II* was first, the beautiful Argentinian racing yacht *Juana*, second, and the British naval yawl *Marabu*, third.

Homeward-bound in the English Channel, *Moyana* ran into a full northwesterly gale and heavy cross-seas which damaged her rigging and opened her seams. The captain decided to safeguard her crew and immediately radioed for help. It came swiftly in the form of the cargo liner *Clan Maclean*, and within minutes *Moyana's* entire crew was safe and the old ketch was left to die in harness.

Denmark's steel, three-masted, full-rigged ship *Danmark* was designed by Aage Larsen and built in the Nakskov ship-yard in 1933. Her gross tonnage is 790. Her mainmast is 130 feet above water level and she carries a total sail area of 1,955 square yards. She has an auxiliary 486-hp diesel engine.

Eighty boys aged fifteen to sixteen participate in six-month cruises, taking courses in all aspects of seamanship to prepare them as officers of the Danish Merchant Navy. Shipowners and the Danish Government subsidize this excellent scheme.

The 790-ton *Danmark*, built in 1933, length 196ft., beam 33ft.

151

The use of sailing craft for pleasure is an ancient one, dating at least to the time of the Pharaohs and resuming, in comparatively modern times, with the Stuart kings of England and their contemporaries in Holland who built most of the royal yachts (from the Dutch 'jacht') of the seventeenth century. Yachting was then a royal pastime and remained one until 1816 when Captain George Crowinshield, an American shipowner of Salem, Massachusetts, introduced an element of democracy by building his *Cleopatra's Barge*. The 'common man' got involved some years later as the pilots and other harbormen around New York, who owned and ran fast-sailing boats as part of their work, began to sail and race for sport. Today millions of people of all classes enjoy the pleasure of sailing.

The yawl has for many years been a popular rig for offshore

The yawl *Islander*, length 34ft., beam 10ft. 9in., which sailed around the world from 1921 to 1925.

cruising and racing.

A famous yawl was *Islander*, built by Harry Pigeon, a farmer from the American Midwest who did not even see the ocean until he was eighteen. He gave her an iron keel weighing 1,250 pounds, a shallow hull, a coach-roofed cabin, extended above the deck, and a self-bailing cockpit, emptied by means of pipes through the hull. She had hand-hewn planks and timbers of Douglas fir, Oregon pine and oak. *Islander* was built in eighteen months at a cost of about $1,100. After acquiring some experience at sea, Pigeon set out alone to sail around the world. He arrived back in Los Angeles on October 31, 1925—to toss the old blue water shellbacks' direst insult, 'Farmer!', back in their teeth.

Another round-the-world sailor was Alain Gerbault, who took the cutter *Firecrest* from Cannes in April 1923 on a voyage of over six years.

Firecrest, length 39ft., beam 8ft. 6in.

153

The famous racing schooner
America, launched in 1851,
length 101ft. 9ins., beam 23ft.

One of the oldest and greatest international sporting events is the competition for the trophy now called the America's Cup, an English silver pitcher which has been in America for over 100 years. It has stimulated the building of some of the world's finest racing yachts.

The first of these yachts was the *America* herself. She was built, at the suggestion of an Englishman, to compete in yacht races held in connection with the first World's Fair. She was designed by George Steers and modeled after some of his pilot boats. Launched in May of 1851, she was delivered in June and shortly sailed across the Atlantic to LeHavre where she refitted for racing. While sailing to the race scene at Cowes, she showed her heels to a fast English cutter, the *Laverock.* As a result, no English yachtsmen would accept the *America's* challenge to a race for 10,000 guineas. She entered a race for 'a cup of limited value' and defeated 15 yachts of the Royal Yacht Squadron on August 22, 1851.

The *America,* sold in England, returned home during the Civil War. She served as a Confederate blockade runner and after being scuttled to avoid capture in the St. John's River, Florida, she was salvaged and served as a Union dispatch boat. After the war she was a yacht again and was one of 23 defenders of 'her' cup against the first English challenge, in 1870. She lasted until 1945.

There have been 20 successful defenses of the Cup, against challengers from England, Scotland, Ireland, Canada and Australia, between 1870 and 1967. Another challenge, from France or England, will be met in 1970. Over $20,000,000 has been spent by challengers so far, and more by the American defenders. The most persistent and beloved challenger was Sir Thomas Lipton, who sent five consecutive Irish *Shamrocks* in quest of the 'Auld Mug' between 1899 and 1930.

The three matches of 1930, 1934 and 1937 were sailed in superb J-boats, the largest racing sloops ever built, and England nearly won the Cup in 1934 with the *Endeavour.* Most of these boats, even the matchless 1937 defender, *Ranger,* were scrapped during World War II and prohibitive costs of replacement have caused the postwar races to be held in smaller 12-meter yachts, the largest class racing today.

The J Class sloops *Endeavour* (*right*) and *Rainbow,* contesting the America's Cup in 1934.

ACKNOWLEDGMENTS

Marine Research Society of Bath, Maine; Mariners Museum, Newport News, Virginia; Massachusetts Historical Society, Boston, Massachusetts; Old Dartmouth Historical Society Whaling Museum, New Bedford, Massachusetts; San Francisco Maritime Museum, San Francisco, California; Smithsonian Institute, Washington, D.C.; British Museum, London, England; Corporation of the City of Aberdeen, Scotland; Italian Embassy, London, England; Missions to Seamen, London, England; National Bank of New Zealand, London, England; National Maritime Museum, Greenwich, London, England; Nederlandsch Historisch Scheerpvaart Museum, Amsterdam, the Netherlands; Royal National Life-Boat Institution, London, England; Science Museum, London, England; Statens Sjohistoriska Museum, Stockholm, Sweden; Trinity House, North Channel Pilots Committee, Harwich, Essex, England; 'Yachting Monthly'.

INDEX

Page numbers in boldface
refer to illustrations.

BOOKS TO READ

The Clipper Ship. A. H. Clark. G. P. Putnam's Sons, 1910. Reprinted by 7 C's Press, Riverside, Connecticut, 1969.

The History of American Sailing Ships. Howard I. Chapelle. Norton, 1935. Bonanza reprint.

The Search for Speed Under Sail. Howard I. Chapelle. Norton, 1967. Bonanza reprint.

The Ship. Bjorn Landstrom. Doubleday, 1961.

Whale Ships and Whaling. Albert Cook Church. Norton, 1938. Bonanza reprint.

On the Spanish Main. John Masefield. Macmillan, 1906.

Queens of the Western Ocean. Carl C. Cutler. United States Naval Institute, 1961.

American Sail. Alexander Laing. E. P. Dutton, 1961.

Fore-and-Aft Sailing Craft. Douglas Phillips-Birt. London: Seeley, Service and Co., 1962.

Some Famous Sailing Ships and Their Builder, Donald McKay. Richard C. McKay. G. P. Putnam's Sons, 1928. Reprinted by 7 C's Press, Riverside, Connecticut, 1969.

Last of the Windjammers. Basil Lubbock. Two vols. Glasgow: Brown Son & Ferguson, 1927–29.

The Wavertree: an Ocean Wanderer. A. G. Spiers. South Street Seaport Museum, 1969.

Sailing Ship Rigs and Rigging. Harold A. Underhill. Glasgow: Brown Son & Ferguson, 1938.

The Way of a Ship. Alan Villiers. Charles Scribners Sons, 1953.

PLACES TO VISIT

Mariners Museum, Newport News, Virginia.

Peabody Museum, Salem, Massachusetts.

The National Maritime Historical Society, Washington, D.C.

The San Francisco Maritime Museum, San Francisco, California.

South Street Seaport Museum, New York City.

Mystic Seaport, Mystic, Connecticut.

Old Dartmouth Historical Society and Whaling Museum, New Bedford, Massachusetts.

OTHER TITLES IN THE SERIES

The GROSSET ALL-COLOR GUIDES provide a library of authoritative information for readers of all ages. Each comprehensive text with its specially designed illustrations yields a unique insight into a particular area of man's interests and culture.

NOW AVAILABLE

SOON TO BE PUBLISHED

GUNS
EXPLORING THE PLANETS
DISCOVERY OF THE AMERICAN WEST
MAMMALS OF THE WORLD
ANIMALS OF AUSTRALIA & NEW ZEALAND
JEWELRY
WARSHIPS
TREES OF THE WORLD
COMPUTERS AT WORK
ARCHITECTURE
MONKEYS & APES
THE ANIMAL KINGDOM
DISCOVERY OF NORTH AMERICA
ENGLISH VICTORIANA
NATURAL HISTORY COLLECTING
MYTHS & LEGENDS OF ANCIENT EGYPT
THE HUMAN BODY
TROPICAL AQUARIUM FISHES
AFRICAN ANIMALS
VETERAN & VINTAGE CARS
MYTHS & LEGENDS OF THE SOUTH SEAS
MYTHS & LEGENDS OF ANCIENT ROME
MYTHS & LEGENDS OF ANCIENT INDIA
ARMS & ARMOR
DISCOVERY OF SOUTH AMERICA